Fools Despise Wisdom
A version of Atheism

By

Ian Cooper

Contents

Introduction 1
  What's the point? 1
Chapter One: Selfishness and Prayer 4
  Prayer as the Voice Within 4
  Bartering with Prayer 7
  The Soul as Currency 10
  Intercessory Prayer 17
  The Lack of Evidence for the Power of Prayer 19
  The Devil and His Motivation 23
  Evidence for the Theological Ineffectiveness of Prayer 27
  Types of Prayer and Meditation 30
Chapter Two: God's Colossal Waste of Time 38
  A God with Too Much Time on His Hands 41
  Love is a Many Evolved Thing 49
  Humans: Not the Perfect Creation 53
    The Nictitating Membrane: 55
    Arrector Pili: 56
    The Tailbone: 57
    Human childbirth: 58
    The Human Mind: 59
  Animals and Design (or the lack of) 63
Chapter Three: Organized Religion's Role in Society 66
  The Rise of the Christian Evangelist: 68
  Divinely-Inspired Atrocities 73

 Failed Expectations 79

Chapter Four: Science and the Soul 85

 Where Are We in Eternity? A Discussion of Heaven and the Soul 85

 How Much Does Your Soul Weigh? A Problem of Mechanism 91

 The Science (and Medicine) of the Soul 97

 Deeper Down the Rabbit Hole 104

Chapter Five: Religion in Business 108

 Businesses as Churches, and Churches as Businesses 117

 Religious ideals in business 121

 Religion and Economics 125

Chapter Six: Replace My Dad with God 132

 Our Parents and Religion 133

 The Social Network 142

 Society and Religion 145

 Aspirational Beliefs and Self Discovery 150

Chapter Seven: Religious Erosion 155

 Erosion of the Church 156

 Erosion of the Practice 162

 Erosion of Mystery 168

 Erosion of the Revealed Texts 177

What's the Point? 184

References 187

Introduction

What's the point?

When I began writing this book, I was angry. Looking back, it's hard for me to say exactly why. I did not, and do not, have a reason to be angry. Being angry is also contrary to my worldview. I am an optimist and tend to look for the best in people rather than focusing on their faults. People's beliefs are their own, and I believe that they should be accountable only to themselves for what they believe. As Thomas Jefferson famously said, "…it does me no injury for my neighbor to say there are twenty Gods or no God. It neither picks my pocket nor breaks my leg (Jefferson, 1788)." So then, why did I write this book?

I wrote this book to explore why I believe what I believe and why I don't subscribe to any religion. I also wanted to express my own personal frustration with modern religious culture. In my twenties, during a period of post-teenage angst, I recall feeling there weren't many atheists out there. It felt like atheists were deplored in political culture, even though the world seemed to have so many problems that were left unsolved by religious thinking. I have since set aside my feelings of superiority, but I felt it was still worth exploring.

My father, who is also an atheist, once told me he felt his generation was dramatically changed by the Moral Majority movement of the 1970s. He felt it was a dividing force and brought religion into politics in a way he hadn't seen before. During this movement, people were forced to take sides between "Right" and "Left" in American politics. Since then, the sides have become increasingly divided and irreconcilable. The Right became attached to a religious framework and became more conservative, while the Left drifted towards a more secularist, progressive movement.

By the time I entered the phase of my life where politics really mattered to me (my early twenties), the left had also become more religious. The trend toward the Left being a more secular party had seemed to abate. Perhaps it was the Carter democrats that began the trend. Perhaps the trend was always there but under the surface. The religious underpinnings of both of the major parties in the United States made it difficult to affiliate with either.

In the end, the only thing that matters about the creation of the material found in this book is what I, and the readers, have taken from it. With that in mind, here is the meaning I discovered while writing this book, either through discussion or the act of researching and writing.

- Helping people to understand your way of thinking is a good thing. Trying to force them to think the way you think is a bad thing and unlikely to work.

- There is no room for militancy in atheism, religion, or anything else in life. Understanding is more powerful.

- People can be good and bad. Religion works as an amplifier. Religion can make good people great and bad people atrocious. I don't think the same is true for atheism.

- Wisdom comes from shutting up more often than it comes from talking.

- I would rather be compassionate and loving than angry and right.

I hope anyone reading this book does so in the spirit in

which I wrote the book - not necessarily in the spirit of understanding and respect, but honesty and forthright communication. Outlined in the following chapters are my thoughts. They represent some of the reasons and justifications for my lack of belief. For some, the ideas may ring true and for others, false. Ultimately, I expect those who are atheists, or who lean in that direction, to find confirmation, while those who are religious will likely find reasons why I am wrong.

I am content with both and welcome the discussion.

Chapter One: Selfishness and Prayer

"There are more tears shed over answered prayers than over unanswered prayers."

Saint Theresa of Jesus

"I have never made but one prayer to God, a very short one: 'O Lord, make my enemies ridiculous.' And God granted it."

Voltaire

Prayer as the Voice Within

If measured by popularity, prayer must be a powerful tool. If it weren't, there wouldn't be so many people across so many religions who practice some form of prayer or meditation. According to the Pew Research Center, 55% of Americans say they pray daily and the same portion say they use prayer as a decision-making tool. Interestingly, 20% of people polled who didn't subscribe to a specific religion said they prayed daily (Lipka & Posts, 2016a). A separate Pew article noted that 3% of atheists pray regularly (Lipka & Posts, 2016b). Luckily, a lot of daily prayer must be occurring inside the heads of those doing the praying. Thought is a perfect mechanism for speaking to God. Think about how odd (and noisy) it would be if 55% of Americans were walking around talking out loud to something invisible. Besides, God's already in people's heads. How else could he monitor our thoughts for purity?

Prayer could have originated as a strange evolutionary side effect of metacognition – the awareness and understanding of one's own thought processes. Each person has an inner dialogue -- When we think, we think with a "voice." This voice has its own intonation and even its own language. Bilinguals sometimes notice their inner voice switching from one language to another, as if there were a second person in their mind translating for them (Blanco-Elorrieta, Emmorey, & Pylkkänen, 2018). Technology has even advanced to the point where we seem to be on the verge of being able to listen in on the inner voice by monitoring neural activity. One day, scientists may even be able to create a translator that will give a voice to people who have no other way of communicating, such as those with locked-in syndrome (Pasley et al., 2012). It's not hard to make the leap from this inner dialogue with oneself, to an inner dialogue with someone else or that there's someone, or something, on the other end receiving the message. It feels right, and I assume people talk to God with this inner dialogue. If people do talk to God using their "brain voice," then it seems safe to assume some talk to their ancestors in this same way. Others may acknowledge they talk to themselves and, occasionally, their "self" answers back.

Some say the inner voice was the precursor of self-awareness. One side of the brain "speaks" and the other side "listens:" A true inner dialogue. There were likely people who assumed the voice they heard was their own and some likely assumed it was God or Gods. This is sometimes referred to as "bicameralism, a term made popular by Julian Jaynes in the 1970s (Jaynes, 1976)."

Ultimately, most of us have an inner voice. What we use that voice for – and who we ascribe that voice to – isn't an issue. What is more troublesome is the distinctions that society makes regarding the social acceptability of that dialogue in our heads. If a response is believed to come from God or another divine source, it is respected and revered.

Many of our revered figures have discussed hearing voices. Gandhi was reputed to have heard the voice of God in his head, which he equated to his inner voice. He once said:

> "For me the Voice of God, of Conscience, of Truth, or the Inner Voice or 'the Still Small Voice' mean one and the same thing. I saw no form. I have never tried, for I have always believed God to be without form. But what I did hear was like a Voice from afar and yet quite near. It was as unmistakable as some human voice definitely speaking to me, and irresistible. I was not dreaming at the time I heard the Voice. The hearing of the Voice was preceded by a terrific struggle within me. Suddenly the Voice came upon me. I listened, made certain it was the Voice, and the struggle ceased. I was calm (Kamath, M.V. Gandhi: A Spiritual Journey. Pg. 116-117)."

Joan of Arc famously heard voices that she attributed to three different angels who spoke for God. She followed the voices dutifully as she believed them to relay the commands of God, though the messages often took interpretation. For years the voices guided her and helped her make her way in life. Eventually, the voices of the saints convinced her of a need to go to battle. She was reported to have said, "Since God had commanded me to go, I must do it. And since God had commanded it, had I had a hundred fathers and a hundred mothers and had I been a king's daughter, I would have gone (Arc & Trask, 1996)." Joan of Arc successfully fought in the Hundred Years' War until she was captured and executed. She was charged with many crimes, but chief among them was her voices, as she refused to acknowledge the voices were not of God (Howse 2008). Today, the voices Joan of Arc heard are thought to have been the results of a form of epilepsy that commonly leads to hearing voices (d'Orsi & Tinuper, 2016).

There is a possibility that much of the religious doctrine throughout history was only doctrine because there were those who accepted the inner dialogue as something divine, but why? Meanwhile, if the responding voice is thought to come from the individual themselves, or a much odder source (like a saucepan or an evil troll) then the individual is considered unstable or insane. And, of course, some have more voices than others. How can people determine if the voice is interior or exterior? Mundane or divine?

Bartering with Prayer

Religious, atheist, or unsure, everyone has this inner voice. The expectations that result from it are what differentiates us. The voice for an atheist comes from the self and has an expectation of rationalism and inward thinking. For a religious person, it may be different. For sure, there are those who have the expectation of divine intervention or favor. There are likely also those who expect a relationship that gets them closer (emotionally) to their deity. There are probably those who feel they must give to their God to receive his favor. The giving comes in the form of bargaining or offering some sort of sacrifice. In Buddhism, meditation and self-denial are intertwined. Sacrifice in service of religion is directly connected to bargaining. When the ancients sacrificed to their Gods, they did it in order to receive a return in the form of better crops, health, or favor in battle. Religious people pray as penance for sin, to barter for forgiveness. Islam highlights the sacrifice and bargaining together.

The Koran, or more accurately the Haddith's version of the night journey, relates a story about a meeting between God and Muhammad where the terms of prayer (sacrifice) were actually negotiated. Muhammad is brought to heaven and God tells him he wants his people to pray fifty times a day. Muhammad mentions this to Moses, who accompanied him on his journey, and Moses tells him that he must go back to God and negotiate a lower number of daily prayers because Man would not comply. Muhammad does this and God lowers the number of prayers by ten. The negotiation continues for a while until the number is reduced to only five. Moses believed five was still too high a number, but Muhammad refused to negotiate any lower (al-Bukhari, 2015).

The story of Muhammad isn't terribly different from the story of Abraham when he negotiated with God in an attempt to save Sodom. In Genesis 18, God is preparing to destroy Sodom for its wickedness. Abraham argues there are still good people in Sodom and asks God if he would destroy the city if there are 50 good people in it, killing the "righteous with the wicked (Genesis 18:25)." God says he would not. Abraham continues to negotiate the number of good people needed to make Sodom worth saving to 10. God agrees.

In a 2013 homily, Pope Francis described Abraham's bargaining with God as courageous and as a paradigm for prayer. He said, "praying is negotiating" and pointed out that those who pray must be tenacious in their prayer. In essence, you must pester God in order to get him to act. Pope Francis said, "if you want the Lord to bestow a grace, you have to go with courage and do what Abraham did." He meant you have to pray persistently in order to get God to take action (Prayer is 'negotiating with the lord,' says Pope 2013).

Like Pope Francis, there are many who feel that, if they pray for a favor, it should be granted by virtue of their belief and ardent devotion alone. They think they are entitled to this favor from God. Others propose a bargain with their deity and offer an exchange to get what they want: "I promise I will never cheat again, just please don't let my wife find out." Here, prayer is used like a barter system: People are purchasing favors from their God with currency, in this case, the assumed currency is the soul. But to what extent are people willing to bargain? There is often a hard limit to what people are willing to give. Why? Every functioning individual innately goes through risk and reward analysis. Even though it surely happens, it is pretty unlikely people will offer things that are excruciatingly painful in exchange for God's favor. Could it also be because they know the likelihood of their prayers being answered is so slim that they are only willing to give things that are of little effort or inconvenience? This is very rational - they limit their offer when bartering, because they recognize the payment in return is unlikely to come.

Of course, when a prayer goes unanswered the pious assume they are failing to understand "God's plan," or that there is some underlying mystery they will never be able to understand. This universal copout is always available and, in this way, faith can be maintained and perpetuated. It turns belief in God into a non-zero-sum game where the believer cannot lose. If their prayer is granted, they win. If their prayer isn't granted, God has some greater plan for them… and they still win.

The Soul as Currency

Heaven is filled with souls and Heaven is the realm of God. God is all-powerful, and so he must only do things by choice. Therefore, God must want to bring all souls to heaven for some reason. God is seeking more souls to stock His realm. This means that the most valuable thing a human can offer to God is her soul, or at least one assumes that souls are God's preferred currency.

It certainly cannot be something material like gold or money -- After all, He can create anything He wishes. Humans have free will and therefore can choose to give their soul to God or not, so God must make it worth their while through favors and answered prayers. So, the soul is a person's bargaining chip.

Bargaining is certainly not solely a Christian phenomenon, and the soul is not the only currency that can be offered. The idea of bargaining may date back to pagan rituals of sacrifice. The sacrifice itself can be seen as a bargain seeking the favor of the Gods by saying: "Here is a hunk of meat, please make my crops grow!" Bargaining may be a wise deal from the perspective of the one who prays, provided God is benevolent. A kind God has the best interest of his people at heart. If the person who makes the bargain doesn't hold up his end of the deal and God is compassionate and understanding there may be no consequences. If, on the other hand, God is vengeful or cruel, the results could be terrifying, equally as bad as making a deal with the Devil. Either way, the pact is an odd one, because one must consider any bargain having a beneficiary on both sides of the deal. We know what the human has to gain from the favor of the Gods, but what does that God stand to gain by collecting souls? Why would God even want to spend the time listening to prayers in the first place? And what, for God's sake, does it mean for God to "want" anything, let alone something as selfish as prayer?

Even if He is benevolent, constant bargaining and asking favors through prayer seems like a very inconsiderate use of a deity's attention. As a parent, I can attest to how irritating it is to have a child who constantly asks for things. Multiply that by billions, and extend the timeframe of this whining to their entire life, and you get an incredible amount of annoyance.

The selfishness plays out in other ways: Imagine a person who prays for a heart to be found for a transplant for his father, so that his father won't die. How could God grant this favor? To do it would mean killing someone. It would mean causing pain to the relatives and loved ones of the donor. The only possible way to save the man's life is through further death and pain. The only caveat would be if God could create hearts at will and give them to those that he deems fit. Setting aside for the moment who He would deem fit and how selfish it would be on the other end to base worthiness solely on who is praying the loudest, why not use that same divine power to place it directly in the patient? Then there is no risk of surgical error and we could get rid of surgeons all together! Why not just let God take over completely? Obviously, God is not just simply materializing hearts into hospitals and inserting them in transplant patients; if He did there would be no doubting His existence… and, as long as one prays, no consequences for any action. If all prayers were answered there would be no disincentive for risky, immoral, wrong-headed behavior or even total inaction, we can all just sit around and let God do everything. That doesn't sound like a life worth living to me.

If God were to intervene, we would be seeing the material results of his direct actions in society and everyone would, logically, be faithful to that God. One could argue that even direct intervention would not prove "God" did it. What if it were simply aliens that are far more advanced than we are? This brings us back to the key point of this book: How can we ever really know? People can believe whatever they choose, but to claim that they know for sure is simply misguided. In the case of a heart transplant, there are at least two definite consequences. The first is that someone else had to die to make that heart available. The person who died would likely have had a family who will be hurt, not to mention the fact that the person had to *die* to provide a healthy heart. The second consequence is that someone else who needs the transplant is not going to get the heart. The person who doesn't get the heart is most certainly going to be distraught and so are his loved ones. In the worst-case scenario, the passed-over transplant recipient may also die as a direct result of not receiving the new heart. How could a person rationalize causing all of that pain by "demanding" that God favor him over all others? How could God be benevolent and agree to make such a deal?

Prayer is about creating a dialogue with someone or something else. A person who prays is asking for assistance or the favor of a God. In effect, he or she is saying, "I would like God to work for me specifically and act as my own personal genie, who may grant my wishes above the wishes of others." There is a definite dichotomy here: Those who are pious and ask for this favor are said to be moral and are praised for trying to connect with their God. Parents even tell their children they are good if they remember to say their prayers each night before bed.

Conversely, those who are "unholy" or desire "bad" things must ask an anti-God, or "devil" to grant their wishes. Who is God or the Devil depends on the perspective of the prayer. Take, for example, a devout fundamentalist Muslim extremist who prays for the destruction of America. He is praying to the same God as Christians, but he asks for something that, if granted, would be called the work of the devil by Christians in the United States. Oddly, when a person prays to God for a favor it's considered good, but if they were to ask the devil for the same favor it would be evil. So then, what is the difference between the acts of these people? Are those that pray actually selling their souls to God as does one who bargains with the devil? In essence, the intent becomes important, but either request comes at a cost and no man, whether assumed pious or not, can be counted on to be benevolent at all times. The Greek philosopher Epicurus noticed this and commented that "If God listened to the prayers of men, all men would quickly have perished: for they are forever praying for evil against one another (Huberman, 2008)."

Returning to our transplant case, what if there is another wrinkle? What if the second transplant recipient was praying to the same God as the first? In this case, they are both praying for the same event to happen. They are both praying, in effect, that another person is sacrificed so that they may live. No matter what, only one person is going to end up getting the heart. In real life, the person who receives the heart is most likely the person who is at the top of the transplant list either because they were on the list first, or they are a better candidate for the transplant. But in a world where prayer actually works, the person that is receiving the transplant was favored by God for some reason or another. Maybe the person that receives the heart worships in a different sect than the other. Maybe, they are Baptist and not Lutheran - would that mean that God prefers Baptists? Maybe the person that received the heart smoked – would that mean that God prefers smokers over non-smokers?

Fortunately, no matter what they say, people don't actually believe that God plays favorites like that or else people would change religions as often as they heard about amazing events. If a person were the sole survivor of a plane crash, everyone would want to know what religion that person is and attendance at his church would go through the roof. The point is that if we believe that God actually favors individuals, then the slope is very slippery.

One may argue that God works in mysterious ways and we cannot understand why he would let one person live and another die, but if his mystery is incomprehensible by man, then the Bible and other religious material must be allegorical. That is to say, God wouldn't clearly tell us what he wants and then go against his own orders. So, the Bible would have to differ by interpretation. If the religious edicts are meant to be translated literally, then there is no mystery in the way that God works. He told you exactly what to do and you must do it.

Clearly, God isn't treating one religion differently than another. God rewards and punishes evenly regardless of the way we pray or it would be obvious which techniques work best. It should be obvious if God favored a particular religion because its adherents would be better off in some noticeable way. Since no religious group seems particularly advantaged, we should conclude that God doesn't have a favorite. God isn't granting the prayers of one group and not the others. Since the right religion is not obvious, God must have made the path unclear on purpose. So, it stands to reason God would discourage any literal interpretation of "his" books and there is no biblically mandated, correct way to pray or, more likely, there is just no God.

Most people don't actually believe that God will act in a direct way to change their plight. They hope that He can help, but most adults know, with some confidence, that He can't or won't intervene directly, even if they won't admit it. Prayers don't generally ask for a new television to materialize in their living room -- instead, a person will phrase their prayers as, for example, a hope for a promotion that will allow them to have enough money to buy the television on their own. Even the religious know that God doesn't make hearts just appear to be transplanted. People only pray for things they know are reasonably likely to happen or that they can influence with their own actions.

There is a phenomenal website that looks at this paradox much closer, www.whywontGodhealamputees.com. The website proposes an experiment to test how much people actually believe in the power of prayer. Someone will first volunteer to be amputated and then a large number of people would be brought together to pray to have God regenerate the volunteer's amputated limbs. So far, this experiment has had no takers because no one thinks God will step in and regenerate the limbs of even the most pious person. The lack of intervention could only mean one of the following: God has a limit and he is incapable of regenerating a limb, God is capable of helping but chooses not to because he doesn't care about big injuries, just the small ones, no one on Earth is truly worthy of the healing, God is not paying attention, or there is no God. I bet you can guess which I think is true.

Praying for relief from major injuries doesn't seem to work and it's equally pointless to ask for help for the small things in life. Epicurus recognized that prayer for intervention is unnecessary when he said, "It is folly for a man to pray to the Gods for that which he has the power to obtain by himself (Huberman, 2008)." Epicurus is making the point that a person's time may be better spent working to accomplish the prayed-for goal. If you want to be rich, use the time that you would have prayed to work, invent, invest or get educated. If you want to be more successful, then spending time improving your relationships may be better. Instead of prayer, your time may be better spent on personal growth.

Praying for "self-improvement" may have some effect on outcomes, but it's only because the person doing the praying gets the benefit of reinforcing their goals on a regular basis. They also get the positive impact of visualization. God didn't do anything to improve their circumstances. They would have received the same benefit from just reminding themselves of their goals every night or morning. In psychological terms, these reminders are called "suggestions." People are suggesting outcomes to themselves when they pray and the act triggers a placebo effect which leads to positive outcomes (Bernard Spilka & Kevin L. Ladd, 2012).

Drive and determination make the dream far more likely to come to fruition than asking an imaginary divine entity to hand it to you on a silver platter. This is not to say that prayer may not have its place as a motivational tool - A good argument could be made for the value of visualization of goals. This visualization can come in the form of prayer. While praying, one can focus on the outcomes that he is seeking and in doing so focus his mind to find ways to accomplish this goal.

Intercessory Prayer

Intercessory praying seeks to *intercede* in the life of a person. The prayer may be for an individual that needs charity or relief or it may be for a person who has died and there is a concern that she won't make it to heaven. It often takes the form of a group praying together for someone. That is to say, people try to influence the heaven or hell decision that God would make by praying for the departed soul. If the person being prayed for is popular enough, the combined voices of all the people praying for him should save him from hell, regardless of the actions of his life. It is a popularity contest and should be considered an extremely egotistical act. After all, it assumes that a group of humans would somehow know better than an all-knowing benevolent being!

A particularly irksome aspect of group prayer for the dead is the assumptions that underlie the process. Those praying seem to think they are a good judge of the person's worthiness to go to heaven, though they would certainly have less insight into the dead person's misdeeds than God. Those who pray may recognize the failings of their departed friend and are hoping to prevent the inevitable outcome. Ultimately, one would expect religious people to leave the decision to the more qualified party, God. If God is benevolent and well informed, there should be no need for intercession.

There is also a perverse incentive when intercessory prayer for the dead is possible. When people believe they can affect the decisions of God with intercessory prayer, they can continue to live their lives however they wish, without consideration of whether their behaviors would cause them to go to hell. They are secure in the belief that they have a group of friends and allies who will intercede on their behalf, because, in this scenario, people are more powerful than God when brought together for a common cause.

New media has taken intercessory prayer to a new low – mass emails and social media posts. Recall any email or post asking you to join everyone in praying, usually for something dramatic. They usually come in the form of:

> Melissa, a 10-year-old girl in Kansas was in a horrible accident. A drunk driver hit her mom's car head-on and the girl has been in a coma for the last 5 days. Please, put Melissa in your prayers tonight, she needs all the help she can get!

If the emails are well written they usually have a heartwarming picture attached. Over the years, I have seen many such messages, but oddly enough I don't think I have ever seen an email that said, WE DID IT! I end up left in suspense. Did the mass email prayer work? Did Melissa wake up? Disturbingly, the people who send the emails must think a large number of voices – regardless of personal relationships to the injured person- will change God's mind about his "plans." If God can hear all prayers, then one voice should be enough. It is selfish to ask people who love you to pray for you and it seems even more selfish to ask people who don't even know you to intercede with God on your behalf. In other words, if you harass God enough, he will act. These e-mails and posts are an attempt to irritate God into action. However, in the end, the people that get irritated most are the people who receive the messages, especially the atheists. And who knows if it even helped little Melissa.

If prayer doesn't work, why keep doing it? Our generation prays quite a bit. According to the previously mentioned (page 7) Pew Religious Landscapes Study, 77% of adults pray at least monthly and 55% pray at least daily. The number declines as the age group gets younger. Only 39% of those born between 1990 and 1996 say they pray daily (Frequency of prayer.; U.S. public becoming less religious 2015). Still, that's a lot of effort put into something that they may not even believe will work! Even if prayer can affect lives, it can only do so in subtle ways – ways that cannot be distinguished from the natural course of life. The emphasis of the next section will be placed on the conclusions that have been made through accepted empirical research by dependable organizations.

The Lack of Evidence for the Power of Prayer

Theist and atheist researchers are actively searching for evidence of God's intercession resulting from prayer. It should be easy to test for verifiable results using scientific methods. Such an experiment could be designed as follows: A group of people suffering from the same illness at roughly the same stage could be split into two groups. The first group, the "intervention" group, would be prayed for, in the hopes that God would intervene and improve their health. The second group would not receive any prayer. Theoretically, if God were listening and intervening, there would certainly have to be a statistically significant improvement in those patients who were being prayed for. Though ethical considerations would require that the afflicted people receive proper medical care, muddying the results slightly, the method of prayer and the denomination of the prayers could be controlled. You could even repeat the experiment with different denominations, to make up for the possibility of a God favoring one sect over another. It could be done.

The key to research like this is in the term "statistical significance," also known as a "p-value." This means that the results of the study have been tested, through impartial mathematical means, to determine the likelihood the results occurred by random chance. As Albert Einstein famously said, "God does not play dice." This is relevant here only because a lot of the research on the benefits of prayer will openly admit that there is no statistical significance to their findings. In a 2009 article published in The Journal of Religion, Wendy Cadge reviews decades of research involving intercessory prayer. In a list of 18 studies, 10 resulted in negative outcomes, 5 were inconclusive or discarded, and the remaining 3 showed minimal or questionable positive impacts (Cadge 2009). If the studies were aggregated, the effect of intercessory prayer would be negative.

The three studies showing a positive impact were highly controversial (Cadge 2009). The first study, performed in 1969, had a very small sample group of only 18 children, which was hardly enough to draw good meaningful conclusions. The second study, published in 1988, showed prayer was correlated with improvements in some categories and negative outcomes in others. In addition, the patients were informed about participation in the study, which could have skewed the results. While the group being studied was larger, the sample groups that showed improvement were often small. For example, the prayed-for group who experienced congestive heart failure was only 8 and the control group was 20 (Byrd 1988). The author of the study aggregated the data to show a statistically significant positive outcome but the results were dubious. The third study was performed in the late 1990s with a sample size of 990 patients and the patients were not informed about their participation. The effects of intercessory prayer were borderline significant, only 3 of the 40 post prayer outcomes showed a positive impact and, on the aggregate, there was no improvement. Additionally, the design of the study was criticized within the scientific community as flawed and had the potential for bias (Hoover & Margolick, 2000). In all three studies, the researchers were Christian and looking for a positive impact. They started the research with a bias.

There are more studies that claim to have found prayer's positive effect, even when the patients themselves had no idea the prayer was being conducted on their behalf. The problem is these other studies couldn't show statistical significance. For example, there was a study performed by the Duke University Medical Center at the Durham Veterans Affairs Medical Center where 150 patients with acute coronary insufficiency were asked to try a variety of alternative treatments (guided imagery, stress relaxation, healing touch, and intercessory prayer). Each patient also underwent coronary stenting, a process in which an artificial structure is placed in a blood vessel to prevent it from closing. The patients were tracked following the procedure to see what complications arose. The report notes that the incidences of complications *were* reduced. Out of the 150 patients that participated in the experiment, the 118 patients who completed the alternative healing programs had fewer complications after their medical procedure was done. This sounds like great evidence at face value. The problem was, as the study admits, the results *were not* statistically significant. The difference between the group who received prayer (and other alternative treatments) and those who did not was not great enough to say that they had any improvement that could be explained exclusively by the prayer. The effects could be from random environmental differences, differences in immune health, better physical conditioning. Since the results weren't statistically significant, the determination that prayer had an effect cannot be made (Krucoff et al., 2001).

This study, like many of its kind, notes the relationship between alternative treatments and healing still needs more study. It is obvious that the researcher would like to believe there is a correlation and therefore wants the search to continue even though the evidence has been found lacking. This is not to say there aren't any benefits to having a positive mental state, but rather, that prayer done for an individual by outside parties has no proven effect.

Theists try to explain the lack of evidence away as God not wanting to present himself, claiming that, if he did so, it would negate free will. That way, followers are free to make the decision, right or wrong. No matter how hard they try they will never be able to show that God is obviously responding to people's prayers. It means that they must have faith. Blind faith - the antithesis to evidence.

Therein lies the problem. With all the religions in the world and all the different ways to pray and honor Gods, how is one to know they are choosing the right type of prayer or even the right religion since God gives no clues to the right answer. We are left to trust what our parents and peers show us as the one true religion. What if it ends up not being the *"one true religion?"* It is a gigantic gamble for believers. If one decides that facing east and kneeling in prayer is the right way to pray, but sacrificing a goat at a temple in Jerusalem is actually the correct way to pray, they have lost all ability to influence their lives through divinity. They will fall out of the favor of God and potentially have to spend eternity in torment. The potential negative outcome is so extreme that it makes no sense that a benevolent God would not share the correct way of praying with all his subjects. After all, a benevolent God would want to save people from suffering. Maybe there is something else at work here - A non-benevolent force.

The Devil and His Motivation

One common response to why there is no solid, irrefutable evidence for the effectiveness of prayer is the devil has a hand in the outcome of the prayer studies. The idea is that the devil, a malevolent entity, will use whatever powers at his disposal to keep man from believing in his counterpart, a benevolent God. The atheist perspective is, of course, the Devil is no more likely to exist than God but this argument is a difficult one to counter. I like to think of the relationship between God and the Devil as opposites: God could be described as the "altruistic devil" and the Devil is the "malevolent God" (the Set, Iblis, Mara, or Angra Mainyu). Before we move on, it is important to look at the Devil or demons and the arguments against them.

Many religious debates discuss the idea that the Devil is causing things to happen. A common theist argument against the age of the Earth is that dinosaur bones were put on Earth by the devil to keep man from believing in God. This is despite there being a glut of evidence contradicting the biblical literalists' view that the Earth is only six thousand years old. If the devil exists and is the cause of many of these happenings (which a truly open-minded atheist should consider as a possibility), then a few fundamental problems surface which need to be resolved:

Is the Devil as strong or stronger than God?

If God is weaker, then what?

Is the Devil not an entity at all, but really our internal impulses, a factor of free will?

Monotheism, or the belief in only one God, is the banner that many religious institutions wave. For Muslims it's, "There is no God but God." For Christians, "Thou shalt have no other Gods before me." Judaism is not so clear. In Judaism, the monotheistic ideal is moved to the second commandment as "You shall have no other gods before Me," and includes the full text of the commandment: "...For I the Lord your God am a jealous God, visiting the iniquity of the fathers upon the children of the third and fourth generation of them that hate Me; and showing mercy unto the thousandth generation of them that love Me and keep My commandments." The Jewish version of the commandant infers other gods exist but their God wants to be above them all. There are scholars who argue Moses believed in many gods, but YHWH was chief among them. There are scholars who argue Jews were always monotheists (God: Biblical monotheism.; Casey Chalk, 2019). We will likely never know.

If it's true that there is only one God, then what station does the Devil hold? If he is strong enough that God cannot control him, then either the Devil is another deity, equal in strength to God, or God is not all-powerful and has at least one fatal flaw - His inability to control the Devil. It falls back to the argument Epicurus made regarding the power of God.

"Is God willing to prevent evil, but not able?
Then he is not omnipotent.

> Is he able, but not willing?
> Then he is malevolent.
> Is he both able and willing?
> Then whence cometh evil?
> Is he neither able nor willing?
> Then why call him God?"

Along the same line as the comments by Epicurus, the existence of a devil should make us question God's goodness. If the devil exists, then hell must exist as well, as the Devil must have a place to dwell. If hell exists as the place where those who are out of favor with God reside, then God becomes a punitive figure. How can we reconcile a God that is both punitive and benevolent?

This dichotomy becomes increasingly more difficult to reconcile the more it is expanded. For starters, what is an appropriate punishment for taboo behavior? To say that my refusal to believe that Jesus Christ is my savior will result in me being punished, intensely, for the rest of eternity seems a bit imbalanced; especially if you, as many Christians do, view Christianity as a religion of love. Let's take this to the next step: If a baby dies before they have a chance to acknowledge the existence and divinity of Christ, what happens to his soul? Surely the baby shouldn't be condemned to hell. What about Purgatory? In any case, does the punishment fit the crime? Do I, as a non-believer who has lived a relatively moral and just life (especially compared to many Catholic priests), deserve a fate worse than death, while a believing murderer or rapist is worthy of forgiveness? If so, can we consider this God to be just?

If God is benevolent and he has created "free will" as the ideal for his creations, then his acceptance of the outcomes of free will would have to go without saying; especially if he is all-knowing. He would have to see the eventuality of people's chosen expression of free will; which would mean that there are those who are condemned before they are born. If God condemns people to hell, then in what sense is there room for the Devil?

In this light, the Devil changes from being a material being to something that is internal. In other words, it is the Devil within God that is the problem, not the Devil as an external actor. If the Devil is not the external actor then in what sense does he control events? Humans are flawed and capable of making horrible decisions, our internal struggle to do right is the struggle between good and evil, that which gives us the impulse to do wrong is the Devil and that which provokes us to do right is God. In the early 1900s (1907 to 1930), Sigmund Freud recognized the inward nature of religion in his explanation of the devil. In his opinion, "God" and "Devil" stem from the human need for a father figure to provide structure and safety. As a broad concept, Freud believed that humans seek a paternal figure and this ultimately led to the creation of religion. He narrowed this by explaining the two competing types of emotion that we feel towards our fathers. Primarily, we revere and respect our father and welcome his judgments and protections. These emotions lead to the creation of benevolent Gods that like to be praised, feared, loved, and respected.

However, we also feel the need to break away from our fathers and forge our own path in life. This defiance and self-assurance are the sources of the Devil and "evil" entities. Looked at in this light, both God and the Devil are internal figures that only have power externally when we allow them to control our actions. Again, this negates the concept of a Devil that acts maliciously to affect our lives and a God that seeks to intervene benevolently. We control our lives and only give power to emotions that we choose to empower - we are the ones in control.

We can then discard the idea that the Devil is meddling in God's prayer-based intercessions in our lives as either a sign of God being fallible or limited. We, as humans with functioning reason, have control over ourselves and our actions. To explain this away with external beings strikes me as a cowardly way to shirk the responsibilities each of us face in our decision making. It is a way to avoid personal responsibility. The Freudian internal battle for self-actualization, in reality, leads to the idea that we are just praying to ourselves and responding to our own prayers - an idea which I like.

Evidence for the Theological Ineffectiveness of Prayer

The idea that we might have a direct line to God is certainly romantic and comforting. Being an atheist doesn't mean that we don't *want* to believe in a world where someone or something has direct control over our existence, will listen to our wants and needs, and intercede on our behalf. It would be wonderful to have some influence on the outcomes of the seemingly uncontrollable events in our lives. Plus, for an atheist, it would be a major relief to know that when we die we do not simply cease to be. Along the same lines, it would be a relief to find out, through quality scientific research, that prayers are being answered by some entity. It would be extremely comforting to know for certain we have a big brother in the sky who watches over and protects us. It would make clear the existence of a God and would at least give some indication of how he would like us to be, and it would answer several key questions: is prayer an effective way to communicate with God? Do religious materials actually expound the benefits of prayer? Is there a pan-religious tenet making it a universal truth that prayer works?

This last question is important because, as there are a multitude of religions and a multitude of sects within those religions. If prayer is effective (even though confirmation is presently elusive to scientists) there would certainly be universal evidence of its effectiveness as a means for calling down divine intervention. It is important to qualify this statement by pointing out that we are discussing prayer, not meditation. If there was a way to consistently ask a being to intervene on our behalf and get results, all religions would have it and all religions would have developed, more or less, the same strategy for their needs, though they may not all have reached that point in the same way.

And yet, even just looking at the traditions of Christianity alone, we don't see this kind of convergence. As is common, there seem to be competing viewpoints in the various books of the Bible. In Psalms 4:4, the Bible recognizes that praying to God is far less important than turning inward. King David (as the writer is assumed to be) beseeches the devout to "Speak in your hearts, and on your beds keep silence." This seems to imply that as long as one's intentions are true; their actions will speak loud enough. If you live a life of good intentions, the all-knowing will know, without you telling him. There would be no need to converse with God directly -- If he wishes to reward you, he knows what you desire and will grant it to you. This seems to be very consistent with the traditional Christian view of God as an all-powerful all-knowing being.

On the other hand, the Bible also makes note of the value

of prayer. Theists often quote Jeremiah 29:11-12 when they argue that God has made it clear through the Bible that his subjects are *required* to pray. The passage says:

> "For I know the thoughts that I think toward you, saith the Lord, thoughts of peace, and not of evil, to give you an expected end.
>
> Then shall ye call upon me, and ye shall go and pray unto me, and I will harken unto you. (Jeremiah 29:11-12)."

This passage is from a letter written by Jeremiah to the people of Jerusalem that were "carried" (abducted) to Babylon. When the entire context of the chapter is taken into account, it is relatively obvious that Jeremiah is asking his people to remain strong and keep their faith, even though their captors may bring them new religious ideas. He tells his people to breed and bear children and be fruitful in the foreign land. Clearly, there was fear that other religions would be extremely attractive and that there was not an innate irresistible pull towards Christianity. The passage was a letter of solidarity with a people that had been forcibly removed from their homeland. Its intent was to hearten them and keep them as members of faith regardless of the influence of their captors. In this light, the passage seems to be cleverly written to give a sense of inward relief despite negative outward conditions.

Like most passages in the Bible, Jeremiah's call to prayer can be interpreted in many ways. This presents a problem for the concept of prayer because the use of the word "prayer" in the Hebrew Bible may have been the result of a mistranslation. Mistranslation is an important part of the debate because too often the strongest justification that theists have for why they pray is that they are commanded to do so by the Bible - a translated text. The Hebrew word *tefillah* has been translated traditionally as prayer but can also be translated as "attachment." In a message such as the one sent by Jeremiah, the meaning could be entirely changed: When God says "Then shall ye call upon me, and ye shall go and pray unto me, and I will harken unto you," he may have meant something more along the lines of "ye shall go and be attached to me." This hardly has the same meaning.

Prayer as a form of bartering is selfish. Intercessory prayer doesn't seem to be effective. The type of prayer sanctioned by Christianity doesn't carry any theological value. Why then is prayer so prominent in all types of religion? There must be some value since it has proliferated so far and so wide. The next section will explore some other types of prayer whose value is more closely linked to scientifically verified outcomes.

Types of Prayer and Meditation

Meditation has been shown to provide a slew of benefits ranging from decreased stress to reducing the effects of aging such as diabetes, cardiovascular illness and immune diseases (Rose, Zell, & Strickhouser, 2020). Probably the most commonly stated benefit of prayer is that of stress reduction. Reduction in anxiety, chronic pain, reduced risk of substance abuse, less obesity, lowered blood pressure, improved immunity and a significantly decreased chance of heart disease are all part and parcel of that reduction of stress. Due to a growing body of quality research, it is clear that there is a direct relationship between meditation and stress reduction; however, the debate is whether prayer also has these benefits. This is intuitive. Most people seem to recognize that if they just slow their minds down and relax, they feel better. So, to piggyback on this intuitiveness, here are some examples of how meditation affects people and how they benefit from it. It is important to remember that there are different types of prayer and meditation. Simply begging God for forgiveness in passing or pleading for help are not nearly the same as imagery focused meditation.

There are many examples of the benefits of meditation. We will focus on the relationship between meditation and physical health, though there are many interesting examples of its effects on mental health and overall quality of life. Meditation has, what seems to be, a wide variety of benefits. In one study, it was noted that patients suffering from atherosclerosis (commonly known as hardening of the arteries) who were taught meditation techniques were significantly less likely to have continued hardening of their arteries. In fact, the study showed that meditators had a marked decrease in arterial thickness, while the non-meditators in the study actually had an increase in thickness. This translated into an 11% (not dramatic but significant) decrease in the risk of heart attacks (Barbor, 2001).

Another study, performed by UCLA, has shown that HIV patients who practiced mindfulness meditation were able to slow the progression of the disease. To be more specific, participants who practiced the meditative technique saw no reduction in their CD4 T cells (a measurement of disease severity) over the course of an 8-week period. The control group that didn't practice mediation saw a decrease in their T cell count. In the end, the researchers noted that the more meditation classes a participant attended, the less likely they were to see a reduced T cell count (Henderson, 2008).

There seems to be a very strong mind-body relationship that relates specifically to health and stress. More stress means worse health and less stress means improved health. Cancer, psoriasis, digestive problems, sleep disorders, heart disease, and other medical conditions all seem to worsen when their sufferer is stressed and improves with reduced stress. In this light, any form of stress reduction can be helpful, but meditation and meditative prayer seem particularly useful.

Now let's look at prayer that acts like meditation. Prayer can be broken down into categories. Most prayer fits into one of the following categories: begging, bargaining, thanks, praise, punishment, remembrance, and prayers of meditation. There can be some interesting overlap in these categories. A punishment prayer, such as the Catholic priest ordering a confessor to perform ten "Hail Marys" as penitence for sin, may involve quite a bit of repetition. This repetition can lead to transcendence. Transcendence in this situation means the prayer is helping the individual reach a mental state that is outside of their normal experience, of clarity of thought or special relaxation. The same can be said of most prayers where the text is prescribed or the method of prayer is preordained, think of the Lord's Prayer. In the West, we are used to images of Muslims praying to Allah by bowing then resting on their heels and reaching to place their hands on the floor. They repeat this action many times. This is, in fact, a preparation for prayer. It is known as *niyya* and is literally the announcement of their intention to pray, not a prayer itself. In terms of meditation, this repetition could be viewed as an engagement of the mind so as to prepare for the *salat*, the Muslim traditional prayer. The *salat* is itself a prescribed chant that could be seen as a form of focused meditation on God, much like the breathing focus of traditional Buddhist and Daoist meditation (Salat: Daily prayers.2009). Judaism has a tradition similar to that of Muslims called Davenening. Davening combines ritualistic prayer and musical vocal intonations. The frequency of Davening prayer is set and the method by which one prays is standardized.

In this light it is easy to describe a difference in the physical changes that take place during prayer versus meditation - For example, if a person reaches a state of calm while praying, they could be said to be meditating, no matter if the prayer is in praise of God or in remembrance of sacred events, like the Catholic rosary. In recent days there is a resurgence of something known as an "archetypal labyrinth." The basic concept of the archetypical labyrinth is that Christians or those of other faiths can experience ritualized meandering, as in physically moving, through the religious events of their holy texts. Through walking and focusing, participants have described reaching a contemplative, or meditative state. In the research, the effects of this meditative walking are veiled in religion and the benefits are carefully worded to avoid a direct correlation to secular mediation, but the whole experience seems to be on par with that of meditation (Karkabi, 2008).

Christianity actually has a more explicit tradition of meditative prayer, which goes beyond the loose correlation above. In the 3rd and 4th centuries C.E., a group of Christians founded a series of monasteries focused on the principles of contemplation and prayer. Members were expected to memorize the whole of the New Testament. Once memorized, the need for Bibles was reduced and it allowed the members to start their contemplations. The expectation was that prayer would become a central part of their monastic life. While they worked, the monks prayed and reflected on specific sentences or passages from scripture. It was very similar to Eastern contemplative meditation.

"When thou are alone…seat thyself in a corner; raise thy mind above all things vain and transitory; recline thy beard and chin on thy breast; turn thine eyes and thy thought towards the middle of thy belly…and search the place of the heart, the seat of the soul. At first all will be dark and comfortless; but if thou persevere day and night, thou wilt feel an ineffable joy (The eclectic magazine of foreign literature, science, and art.1852)." Does this sound like advice from the Dali Lama or a 14th-century Christian monk?

The later leaders of this movement, Antony, Athanasius, and Pachomius focused on solitary prayer that was intended to allow the performer of the prayer to transcend Earthly wants and gain a heavenly perspective. This perspective is very similar to that which is sought in the Buddhist meditative tradition, but with Christian undertones. These "Fathers of the Desert" were known for their asceticism (self-denial and discipline) and hard-working ways, but mixed into this tradition was reason and contemplative thought. The Desert Fathers even referred to their prayer practices as meditation (Allies, 1896). Pachomius of the Thebaid, one of the founders of the movement who was later canonized, taught his followers to "meditate" continuously during their work. Meditation to Pachomius meant continuous recitation of the word of God (Veilleux, 1980).

The Hesychasts, a word that was used to refer to the "quiet" and contemplative lifestyle that the monks led, were a group of Christians that used meditation to seek out the "mystic and ethereal light" of God. They recognized the physical and emotional benefits of Eastern style meditation in the 1330s and were a relatively powerful group for many years. Their doctrine of an ethereal light became an article of faith for the Greek Christian community in 1351 and was viewed as something that differentiated the Greek Orthodox Church from the Roman Catholics.

Less than 100 years later, Thomas A' Kempis wrote the Imitation of Christ, which helped guide an ascetic lifestyle and also expounded the values of contemplative meditation and the value of focusing on the "interior life." He rationalizes this by invoking a passage from the Bible; "The kingdom of God is within you (Luke 17:21)." His followers are encouraged to, "learn to despise outward things, and to give thyself to inward things (à Kempis, 1418)." By practicing their inward meditations, Kempis says, they are able to get closer to God. Kempis' argument is so strong that it is accepted by the Catholic Church and his book becomes one of Catholicism's great works.

These days, there are Christians that are seeking to join the meditative traditions of other religions and cultures with their own in an effort to improve the benefits of prayer. Some of these attempts are more successful than others. For example, there is a growing group of Christians that are practicing a form of yoga. It has been referred to as Christian Yoga, Holy Yoga, and Yahweh Yoga. The practice of traditional Hindu yoga is being changed to bring in Jesus and the teachings of the Bible. There are obviously detractors on both sides of the religious divide. Hindus don't like to see their sacred poses altered and renamed to fit an entirely different religion. Christians, especially Catholics along with the Pope, have difficulty reconciling rituals of Hinduism that are meant to salute Hindu Gods with their own belief in a single specific God. This possible commandment breaking exercise is just too close to idolatry for many people. Regardless of the protest, the practice of Christian yoga continues to grow.

This is the strength of religion. It can integrate aspects of other religions and cultures over time to draw in converts. Similar to the celebration of Christmas and Easter, which were at one-time pagan holidays and have now been adopted by Christian culture.

There is also a compelling argument that simply repeating the "Our Father" prayer from the Catholic tradition could be viewed as meditation if it is done correctly. The meditation tradition has been with Christianity since the earliest days of the church.

Islam has a measure of meditative prayer as well. In moments of crisis, a Muslim is expected to recite the shahadah, a mandated prayer. It is so revered in the Muslim community that the recitation of the shahadah is one of the "Five Pillars" of Islam. In a moment of stress, Muslims are encouraged to take a step back and say, "There is no God but Allah; Muhammad is the messenger of Allah." If done correctly it should calm a raging man, ease the pain of women during delivery, and focus an anxious student. This recitation can be seen as tantamount to mediation, a way of stepping back from a stressful situation and to refocus the mind on something else. It is no different than counting to ten repeatedly when you are angry. The results of this could easily match the results of a well-performed meditative act that relieves the stress of the meditator.

What is it that draws people to prayer? Hope is a powerful emotion and the need for security may be even more powerful. The thought that there is a being who can cure your woes and infinitely improve any situation gives hope, a being who is capable of keeping a person safe in any situation. Logically, one would need to communicate his concerns to this being. Prayer is one way to do so. I am not a scholar on the subject, but I would venture a guess that religion is simply responding to the needs of its community for hope and security. Providing a sense of hope and security is a great quality of religion, but it's only great until it leads to a dogma or ideology that impedes the growth of mankind or causes pain to the innocent.

Our flaws as human beings are the only reason, we need a sense of hope and security. Humans pray in an attempt to reduce the pains caused by our "design" or lack of design. There would be no need to pray if we weren't haunted by diseases and infirmity. No bargaining for souls would be needed if there were no need for the afterlife. We are so imperfect we invented Gods as coping mechanisms. Clearly, our lack of design shows either a lack of a designer or one who is incompetent.

Chapter Two: God's Colossal Waste of Time

"If God has cable, we are the 24-hour doofus network."

Will Durst

"If it turns out that there is a God, I don't think that he's evil. But the worst that you can say about him is that basically he's an underachiever."

Woody Allen

As humans, we navigate the world through our experience of being human. In an attempt to understand this world, we give human traits to things that are not human and, more so, to those things that we recognize as having some sort of intelligence. Think of how we talk to our pets or try to convince a golf ball to go down the fairway (get legs!). This is known as anthropomorphism or humanization, and it is deeply ingrained into our culture - and highly popular. For example, television shows like "Meerkat Manor" survive specifically because people love the concept of animals acting like humans. They may not look like us, but they are presented as being just like us. Some animals show remarkable human-like behavior. There have been movements to treat certain animals as non-human persons. Dolphins, for example, are incredibly intelligent and exhibit behaviors such as tool usage, empathy, and self-awareness.

Researchers, animal activists, and the general population have debated the ethics of keeping dolphins in captivity for years (Richard Monastersky, 1999).

God and the Devil, despite being omnipotent and omniscient are not immune to being viewed through this human lens - in popular movies such as "Oh God! You Devil" (1984) and "Bruce Almighty," (2003) God is turned into an altogether human entity. The concept sells. Of course, this goes beyond movies. Statements like, "God is listening" infer that he has human-like ears. The Bible often speaks of God in a human context, with basic human emotions such as anger and want, joy and sorrow. This is all a form of anthropomorphism. A passage from Deuteronomy illustrates this perfectly:

> "You shall not bow down to them or worship them; for I the LORD your God am a jealous God, punishing children for the iniquity of parents, to the third and fourth generation of those who reject me, but showing steadfast love to the thousandth generation of those who love me and keep my commandments."

I highlight the above text for the implications it has on atheism. If the passage is read literally, my grandchildren's grandchildren will be punished (even if they are moral people or devout theists) for my inability to believe in His existence. More importantly, though, what apart from a human can experience jealousy? It does not make sense for an all-powerful deity to be subject to such a lowly and short-sighted emotion. What or who can an all-powerful deity possibly be jealous of?

It is possible that this passage refers to the existence of other Gods. In fact, there is a long history of that being the accepted case. The Gnostic gospels revealed that some early Christian leaders and sects, as early as the 1st century of the current era, believed that the creator of the Earth was not the only God, nor was he the strongest. They also believed the God that created Earth was malevolent. By their logic, the Christians who worshipped Him were deluded and destined to be out of the favor of the "true God," the progenitor of that creator God (Pagels, 1979).

Countless other passages in the Old Testament refer to God as if he were some sort of wizened old man, with all of the flaws that come with it. Take, for example, Genesis chapter three where God walks with Adam and Eve in the Garden of Eden after they have eaten from the tree of knowledge. This passage describes God strolling - walking as a human would - through Eden. It even goes as far as to say that God cannot see Adam because Adam is hiding (Genesis 3:8-11). If God is all-knowing and all-seeing, as many Christians believe, then how can Adam hide?

Later in the Bible, Jeremiah, when describing his conversations with God, refers to a God that "put forth his hand and touched my mouth (Jeremiah 1:9)." He interacts with God on a distinctly human and physical level. Later he even quotes God as saying, "I myself will fight against you with an outstretched hand and with a strong arm." With infinite power at such a being's disposal, why use a mere hand?

If the Christian Bible (or the holy book of any Abrahamic religion for that matter) is to be taken as literal or even to some extent allegorical, one must then assume that God has human traits. Ironically, a God with human-like traits would lend credence to the idea that God created man in his image, imperfect and limited. So, let us explore what it would mean for creation if God is all-knowing, all-powerful, and yet acted as though he were human. Let us see his "effort" and "reasoning" as it relates to creation and the structure of the Universe around us.

A God with Too Much Time on His Hands

To understand an atheist position on Intelligent Design it is necessary to fully understand the different positions that exist on both sides. There are two separate arguments, though they share some common ground. The first argument (and ironically the least complex one) revolves around what is known as "Irreducible complexity." The second delves into the complexities of love.

The argument of Irreducible Complexity is common among Christians. The basic tenet of the argument is that when something is very complex it takes a designer to fashion it. It is akin to saying, "I believe in God because there is no way that something as beautiful and complex as the human eye could have happened by accident." By extension, anything that is sufficiently complex must be the product of an intelligent creator. This is often the credo of "Intelligent Design" advocates, but it is relatively easy to rebuke. After all, just because one cannot understand how something complex works or how it came about, does not make it of supernatural origin.

Irreducible complexity is a common argument against evolution. The major tenet of this theory is that if one part of a complex system were removed or non-functioning then the system itself would cease to function. For example, if a cog were removed from a watch, the watch would not continue to tell time - the watch must be whole. One extremely common example that proponents of this theory use is the human eye. What use, they say, is a human eye that is missing a major part like a pupil? If the eye was not made by a designer but was instead evolved through random mutation, then important parts such as the pupil, lens, rods, and cones in the eye might not be present at a given stage. Or, if they were, they would not be optimal for sight. If the eye was not developed exactly as it is, in-whole, these theorists ask, wouldn't it be completely useless? It follows from this logic that the only possible explanation for the creation of the human eye would be a designer who made it just-so. It is, they claim, an irreducible system. Except, of course, the eye is a terrible example, but I will explain that later.

Examples aside, there are many problems with irreducible complexity. Looked at from the atheist point of view, the first problem is that it is an argument from incredulity. Simply because we do not understand an idea or theory does not mean that it's magical. I have no real understanding of how Bluetooth technology works, as I imagine many people do not. Bluetooth connections cannot be seen or felt. They are wireless even though they connect devices to each other and allow them to communicate, such as a headset to a cell phone or the remote control to a Sony Playstation console. Someone could attempt to explain how Bluetooth technology works to me and it would go over my head. They would be forced to use terms with which I am not familiar, such as "spread-spectrum frequency hopping (Franklin & Layton, 2000)." Each new piece of information would lead to new questions. I would need to invest a fair amount of time to gain an understanding of the way Bluetooth works, which can be off-putting. Even then, that would likely not be enough for me to truly understand it.

Simply because I do not understand how life could have been created from nothing, how Bluetooth works, or how an eye could have evolved, does not mean it was done supernaturally. Instead, my lack of understanding is the result of ignorance on the topic. Though things may seem too complex to have evolved, there may be additional information that can shed light on the problem. In other words, research. Such is the case with the human eye - and here I will explain why the human eye is a poor example of perfect design.

The argument from irreducible complexity requires assumptions. One must assume that irreducibly complex parts have had no alternative uses and could not have had any precursory steps. For example, an eye that can simply discern light from dark could be useful, though not for reading. I am not an expert in evolutionary biology, but a rudimentary eye seems like something that is easily evolved from cells sensitive to light. Light and dark vision may not be as complex as the eye of a human, but it would still be useful to many different organisms and help them survive. Vision of this type may have been, in fact, a beginning step toward the current version of the human eye. The next step in evolution would be for a group of these light-sensitive cells to be able to improve light and dark detection. These cells would be useful in many ways, but possibly the easiest to recognize would be to tell if it is night or day. Or, alternatively, if the organism has found a hiding place that shelters it from light. It could be the difference between the appropriate time to hunt or hide from your predator. If the cells were then to recess into some sort of fold or socket in the body, very slightly with each mutation, over many generations the organism would be able to determine the directionality of light. Again, the uses of this are relatively apparent - knowing the direction of light lets an organism track prey and predators better. The deeper the recess, the easier it would be to determine directionality.

The recessing would continue until a small hole or tunnel lies between light-detecting cells at the back of the cup and the outside world. With a small hole, it becomes possible to gain a rough outline of an image as the light through the hole lands on the light-sensitive cells at the back of the recess. The next likely step would be towards focusing the light onto the cells. At this point, there would likely be translucent or transparent tissue that covers the pinhole and protects these cells from damage - focusing the light might be as simple as a mutation that thickens the middle of this tissue and thins the edges. The tissue that covered the pinhole would start to squeeze and become thicker in the middle and thinner at the edges. As this continues, a lens would develop, allowing the eye to gather more light and focus the image more clearly on the light-sensitive cells. The final step is for muscles controlling the skin (such as for shivering, movement, or protection) to also control the thickness of the lens. A mutation that causes such a muscle to attach to the lens itself and expand and contract it depending on environmental conditions would be very advantageous. The last step is the development of the aperture of the eye, also known as the pupil.

Let's stop there for now - What I have just described is simplistic and lacking in many steps, but it is, unmistakably, an evolved eye. For ease of translation, I have done quite a bit of condensing and a good amount of step-skipping (Ridley, 1996), but Charles Darwin, and many others since, described exactly how the eye might have evolved using light/dark cells as a beginning step (Darwin, 1859). Computer models have also shown that it is possible to evolve the human eye in as few as four hundred thousand generations (Dawkins, 1995). Four hundred thousand generations may seem large in human terms, and technically it is - assuming that a generation takes about 20 years, it would only take eight million years - greater than recorded human history. But, of course, the eye did not develop in a static human. It first developed in lower-order creatures and evolved alongside them. If these early eyed creatures were fish-like and had new generations annually, then they could have potentially evolved - with the right environmental conditions - functional human-like eyes in less than four hundred thousand years. From a geological perspective, this is a barely-visible span of time. Very possible.

Regardless, it is clear the eye can evolve and it is *not* irreducibly complex. It seems even simpler to understand the eye than to understand how Bluetooth works. This may simply be my ignorance again, but the parallel to incredulity is clear.

There are those who would argue that we have not *seen* new body parts evolve, though we have. They say that there is some leaping necessary, for example, the light-sensitive cell has to show up in one generation for the whole system to evolve. There are examples of sudden genetic changes in the world around us. My favorite example, though not perfect, is that of my sister-in-law's cat. The creepy cat has an extra toe. He has a condition called polydactyly, which can be inherited from the cat's parents or could be the result of a mutation in a gene that regulates toe growth. The trait is also dominant, increasing the likelihood it will be passed to the next creepy cat generation. A toe is certainly not a limb or cells, but the cat already enjoys abilities other cats do not. I have seen the cat pick up toys and food as if it has an opposable thumb. Seeing it is actually slightly eerie because the way that it manipulates objects feels almost human. One could easily understand how this extra toe would produce an evolutionary advantage, especially in a situation where there has been a dramatic environmental shift that limited the number of animals reproducing.

The reason this topic is relevant in a chapter on how God wastes time is that it actually highlights an interesting argument that can be made about complexity. The argument requires ignoring the true definition of irreducible complexity and instead focusing on what it means to have complexity.

Complexity can take many forms. There is organic complexity, which can be seen in the human eye and there is inorganic complexity like the Universe in which we live. Both are equally strong in refuting the existence or usefulness of God. One need only ask, why does everything need to be so complex?

Does the human eye or even the Universe *need* to be so complex? The answer is no. With our limited human knowledge and capacity, we can easily think of improvements to both systems. There are plenty of "creations" that are unnecessarily complex and none that are irreducibly complex. The argument that results from only unnecessary complexity is very similar to the argument made by Epicurus. Is God incapable of designing simple systems? If he is capable, does he not wish to create simple systems or in other words, is he a joking tinkerer? If he is capable and wishes to, then why do the unnecessarily complex systems exist?

A theist may say that God is simply working within the rules of the natural environment that he created. The environment was his intention and the resulting systems simply evolved from it. Again, this belies literal interpretation of the Bible and other texts, but more importantly, it tells us that God has limits (even if those limits are self-imposed). God is limited by the laws of nature. God cannot get rid of gravity or make water compressible, because he cannot act against the laws of nature. Arguments that propose God as the "prime mover" (i.e. the being that kicked off the Big Bang) emphasize God creating the "physics" by which our Universe operates. He set the plan in motion. If God was only the prime mover and cannot act after the initial creation, prayer, worship, dogma, and holy texts must all be creations of man. If God can't alter his creation, then in what sense is God all-powerful?

Biblical literalism provides great fodder for a religious debate because their God does things in unnecessarily difficult ways. One of my favorite claims is that the devil (I have also heard God did this as well) placed dinosaur bones in the Earth to fool humans into believing the biblical claims of creation are false. Of course, this assumes an extremely powerful second deity (the devil-as discussed earlier) which would dash the concept of monotheism. More importantly though, deviously placing dinosaur bones would be an incredible waste of time and effort. God has control over all creations, including the Devil, and would have no problem preventing his mischief, but instead, he allows the devil to play a gigantic joke on the people who he so loves. Maybe God is incapable of controlling the Devil, in which case we could easily make the argument it is just as likely that the Devil made the Bible to throw us off the true path to God.

In the end, though the big question would be why mess with dinosaur bones in the first place? Why add complexity to a situation when the absence of fossils would be a great benefit to the faith of his people? Certainly, it would be much less work to just leave these bones out of the picture completely.

Another argument along the same lines has to do with the Universe itself. If God designed the entire Universe, why did he make it so big? The size of the Universe is unfathomable to humankind. Scientists have made some extremely accurate measurements and have come to the conclusion that the Universe likely contains around 1.6×10^{60} kilograms or about 1.6 trillion trillion trillion trillion trillion kilograms (Nielsen, 1997). The number could also be stated as 1.6 million million million million million million million million million million. Would it have mattered to your understanding if I had removed or added a trillion when transcribing the number above? The number is so large we can't even conceptualize what it means. We could never hope to know all the matter in the Universe. There is simply too much. From a theistic point of view, the incredible quantity of matter was created by the same God who created Earth and Mankind. Why? Maybe he just wanted us all to see a sparkly sky. It would have been easier to string diamonds around the planet; it would certainly take less matter.

If we are God's favorites and are created in his image, he certainly went through a lot of trouble to ensure we understand how small and unnecessary we are in the Universe. After all, God would not have created man, given us laws to live by, and given his only son (if you are Christian) if we were not extremely important to him. So why did he create so much stuff in the Universe we, for whom the Universe was created, have no way of accessing or even understanding? We cannot even see all of the galaxies, much less all the stars in the Universe with our best technology.

The best explanation I can think of is that God must have too much time on his hands, or doesn't exist at all.

__Love is a Many Evolved Thing__

The second argument for Intelligent Design is love, and human understanding of ourselves: our self-awareness. To put it differently, can one define love? How can evolution account for something that we cannot even put into words? Why would love exist if there is no God? In essence, the argument is that something as complex, indescribable, and enthralling as love would not occur without the intervention of the divine. Love is often touted as something we cannot see, touch, or explain. Yet it is also a feeling that we all recognize and rarely debate. Theists liken it to their belief in God. To them, it is the emotion of meditating on God, or even is God manifest. They say that each person experiences it differently, and so the definition of love is mystical and difficult to pin down. This is a compelling argument.

For the purposes of this discussion, Miriam-Webster's dictionary definition of love will be used. Love is "affection based on admiration, benevolence, or common interests (Merriam-Webster Online Dictionary, 2009)." This definition is broad enough to encompass spousal, parental, and friendly love. I don't want to rationalize love in the same way an atheist attempts to rationalize religious belief. It is invisible, like God, but we do not doubt its existence because it is something all of us (hopefully) have experienced personally. I think back to countless conversations that I have had on religion and I find it odd that I have not had anywhere near the same amount of conversations on the topic of love and emotion. It is as though people accept love as a personal, indefinable force and we nearly never question it. Albert Einstein once asked, "How on Earth are you ever going to explain in terms of chemistry and physics so important a biological phenomenon as first love?" And yet we actually can.

The argument for the complexity of love as proof of God can only stand if it meets two criteria. The first is that it cannot be shown to have evolved. The second is that it cannot be explained biologically. If love can be shown to be evolutionarily beneficial and chemically or biologically explicable, then there is no need for God as an explanation.

The evolutionary basis for love is, in many respects, intuitive. Imagine a set of organisms where group cohesion is extremely important for survival and reproduction. These organisms are physically weak and their young are not capable of supporting themselves until a late age. For the species to survive in a difficult environment, it would be necessary for the group to work together in order to hunt effectively and protect themselves. The children of the group would need to be protected and the pair bond between parents would need to be particularly strong. Over generations, those individuals within the community who were able to form stronger bonds would survive better and have more offspring. Love causes individuals to act in ways that serve others rather than themselves, even to the point of the ultimate self-sacrifice. As Frans De Waal put it, "Human societies are support systems within which weakness does not automatically spell death (De Waal, 2005)." Both the relationship within the family and within the community would be well served by adding love to the equation - it is an excellent adaptation.

Charles Darwin pointed out, in *The Descent of Man*, humans are not the only animals who have an inclination to love. He points to one animal seen around humans all the time, dogs. He said, "The love of a dog for his master is notorious; in the agony of death he has been known to caress his master." More poignant were his observations about monkeys and their feelings of maternal love. Darwin notes it is common for a mother monkey to be so affected by the loss of a child they themselves would die (Darwin, 1871). In apes, empathy and maternal love are apparent. In 1996, a three-year-old boy fell into the gorilla exhibit at the Brookfield Zoo in Chicago. The child was injured and at risk of being attacked by aggressive male gorillas. A mother gorilla found the child and carried him to safety at the other side of the enclosure. The female gorilla cradled the child, rocking him until the zookeepers were able to come and get him out (Gorilla at an Illinois Zoo Rescues a 3-Year-Old Boy, 1996). I would challenge anyone to watch a video of this event and not recognize it as love.

A biological explanation of love may seem callous, taking away some of the dewy-eyed luster from a very complex emotion. I do not think, however, that acknowledging love as a biological function diminishes it. It certainly doesn't change the way I feel towards my wife or children - I still love them, and I am happy to love them. Like many complex things, including the human eye, love is something to be cherished regardless of whether we know the mechanism by which it operates, just as I am happy for my sight. We are beginning to understand the mechanisms of love in the human body. What was once the realm of uncertainty and mysticism is quickly becoming as describable, biologically, as digestion and reproduction.

We know, now, that complex chemical interaction and electrical signaling are found at the very foundation of love. In 2004, researchers tracked blood flow, and by inference the chemicals, in the brains of subjects who reported being "madly" in love. The researchers determined two major factors in the feelings associated with passionate love, and their findings were very telling. Dopamine, a chemical used in our brain's reward systems, was the first factor and was found to be present in high quantities. Intense levels of dopamine are associated with "focused attention as well as fierce energy, concentrated motivation to attain a reward, and feelings of elation - even mania - the core feelings of romantic love (Fisher, 2004)."

The second factor involved increased activity located in the area of the brain known as the Basal Ganglia, which is often referred to as the "reptilian brain" or R Complex. Within the Basal Ganglia, the caudate nucleus is one of the oldest parts of the brain, associated with basic needs and - again - our internal reward system. The more passion a subject reported the more activity was observed in the caudate nucleus. This region of the brain is usually more linked to voluntary movement, but this study and others have found that it is also linked to social behavior. For instance, the caudate nucleus was active when researchers studied how people treated others who violated or broke social norms (say, for example, a corrupt politician). Activity in the caudate nucleus increased when someone was about to be punished. The more severe the expected punishment, the more activity was found in this region of the brain. This relationship between the "movement" part of the brain and "social activity" is thought to help explain the phenomenon of road rage: People reacting to the breaking of a traffic norm feel so strongly that the offender should be punished, that they will put themselves and others in harm's way (Restak, 2006)!

Many researchers have described how love and other emotions could evolve. I do not mean to devalue love. I don't think that love will ever be explained away. It is the sensation that people gain from love that matters, which will not change as we learn how and why it works. The point is, the two criteria that would refute God as being needed for love - that it can be evolved and that it can be physiologically understood - have been met and the arguments are only improving over time. Love does not require God to exist.

Humans: Not the Perfect Creation

Omniscience infers the ability to see all possible outcomes, and a deity that does not have omniscience is extraordinarily dangerous. Think of a child who, in an effort to look at what is in a frying pan, is willing to place his hand on the burner. Since the child does not understand how the stove works, the decision to put a hand on a burner seems logical, even wise. It does, after all, allow the child to peer over the edge and see what is in the pan. As we grow older, however, we learn more about the world, about how touching the burner will hurt us, and find better ways to see what is in the pan. Though we gain knowledge and techniques over time, we are never fully aware of all possible outcomes. We have no way to tell, in advance, what is in the pan if we aren't the ones who put it on the burner. If God does not have omniscience then the decisions he makes may be much like that of the child in the example. He may be missing a critical outcome of his action. God becomes a curious tinkerer. God makes mistakes. God gets burned.

If God was omniscient or, at the very least interested in our well-being, he would have designed us, and everything around us, to the best of his ability. Which he certainly did not. Is God a poor engineer, does he have attention deficit disorder, or are our design flaws an expression of His malevolent will? As Gary Marcus put it in his book Kluge:

> "Perfection, at least in principle, could be the product of an omniscient, omnipotent designer; imperfections not only challenge that idea but also offer specific forensic clues, a unique opportunity to reconstruct the past and better understand human nature (Marcus 2008, 16)."

Marcus' point is that perfection would be an indicator of a creator because it is so rare in nature. Conversely, imperfection is a direct refutation. The only time it would not refute the existence of God is if God either did not care or was not capable of perfection. In other words, a perfect creator must be motivated to create something imperfect. A perfect God that intentionally designs a being with imperfections must be malevolent or, as Woody Allen suggested, an underachiever.

Why create a human so that birth is so incredibly painful and dangerous for women? Why create a back that is so poorly designed that it causes pain in roughly one-quarter of the human population (Deyo, Mirza, & Martin, 2006)? Why do so many parts of nature, and the human body, seem to be leftovers?

These leftovers, also known as vestiges, are a clear

indication of an evolutionary process. As defined by Merriam-Webster's dictionary, a vestige is:

> 1: a trace, mark, or visible sign left by something (as an ancient city or a condition or practice) vanished or lost

> 2: a bodily part or organ that is small and degenerate or imperfectly developed in comparison to one more fully developed in an earlier stage of the individual, in a past generation, or in closely related forms

The implication is that a vestige leads to answers about something in the past, just as ruins might lead to clues about an ancient culture. The evolution of humans has produced some interesting, funny, and notable vestiges. There are countless examples of human and non-human vestiges but I will now go over a few that, in my opinion, are the most fun.

The Nictitating Membrane:

In the corner of the human eye, closest to the nose is a small fleshy triangular-shaped piece of skin. This bit of tissue is the remnant of an organ called the nictitating membrane. This membrane is a legacy from the past and could be called a third eyelid. The eyelids on humans pass over the eye vertically, they go up and down. This third eyelid actually moves horizontally in the animals who still have them, from side to side, and can be used for a few interesting things. Birds, reptiles, amphibians, and some mammals still have this third eyelid, which they use to clear debris and protect their eyes from contaminants. In some underwater animals, the membrane is transparent and protects the eye while allowing the animal to see, much like a pair of goggles. Unfortunately, humans must buy goggles and protective eyewear - the nictitating membrane has atrophied and all that is left is a useless flap of skin in the corner of the eye (Drummond, 1897). Why would God not install such an important feature, leaving our eyes vulnerable to contaminated water and dust? Did he give it, then take it away, but still leave a little bit in the corner to remind us of what we lost whenever we close our eyes to protect ourselves in an over-chlorinated pool?

Arrector Pili:

Another example of a human vestige, (and certainly my favorite as a man of Italian descent) is part of the human body known as the arrector pili. The arrector pili are under the skin of mammals and perform only one function, standing hair up. When a human gets a chill, the resulting goosebumps raise the hair and are a result of arrector pili. So, what purpose does standing hair serve? There are a couple of different possibilities, both of which have great implications for the more hirsute of us. The first is that it is a vestige from a hairier time when warmth was in short supply and body hair was essential. When a cold breeze would pass, the arrector pili would push the hair up and trap the warmer air leaving the body which would provide additional insulation. As humans lost hair, the arrector pili became obsolete, but still blindly functioned.

The second possibility, and the one that I favor strictly for humor purposes, is that it is a defense mechanism (Roberts, 1986). Anyone who has a cat will recognize this use of the arrector pili. When you spook a cat, their fur stands on end which has the effect of making them look larger. In other words, they puff up. In humans, the same response mechanism may exist. Imagine a hairy, maybe Austin Powers-like figure, getting angry and his every individual body hair standing on end to make him look larger. What a great picture of a vestige that is! Arrector pili may clearly show a God with a sense of humor, but the question will always remain. Why?

The Tailbone:

Not all vestiges are benign. Sometimes they cause serious problems. The tailbone, technically known as the "coccyx," is one such vestige. The coccyx consists of three to five vertebrae at the base of the spine, likely the remnant of a tail. Our ancestors were tree climbers and used a tail to help them balance. Walking didn't require a tail, and it eventually faded away. The tail never fully disappeared, however, and we bear the remnants. Interestingly, humans are neither the only ones with a tailbone nor the apes with the most de-evolved tails. Gibbons, for instance, have been able to whittle their tail down to just one or two remaining vertebrae (Campbell, 1998). The coccyx is a source of pain for many people. It is not difficult to injure; it is as easy as sitting down for some. Once it is injured it causes some relatively serious issues. Besides the pain itself, injuring the tailbone can make it difficult to sit (Hertling & Kessler, 2005). A terrible design flaw.

Either these vestiges show God's malevolence and childlike sense of humor, his imperfection, or they show that God did not design man. Religion itself may also be a vestige of earlier human culture. It may be that religion grew from a need for group cohesion. By creating a group of individuals with shared beliefs, the group cooperates more effectively and survives better than one that does not share the same beliefs. Ultimately, successful ideas are passed on from generation to generation. There may even be a religious gene. In the 2015 book "God is Watching," Dominic Johnson said theists were rewarded for their cooperation and were less likely to upset their fellow humans (Johnson 2016). I can relate. Sometimes atheists can be insufferable, but then again, so can everyone.

Human Childbirth:

What would being created in God's image mean for our physical and psychological makeup? What it may mean is that humans were made as well as God could make us. There are no possible improvements. Bertrand Russell once said, "I cannot but think that Omnipotence operating through all eternity might have produced something better (Russell, 1957)." It would seem God is either exceedingly imperfect himself and incapable of creating perfection or is unconcerned with our design and unwilling to build us as well as he could. As we learn more about how we, and our closest relatives, the apes, work, our poor "design" becomes more and more obvious.

Primatologist Frans De Waal, in his book "Our Inner Ape," noted that people seem to be stunted in evolution. Through our innovation, humankind has successfully removed selective pressure (De Waal, 2005). For example, Frans De Waal proposes that the trouble women have during childbirth is the result of this lack of selective pressure. He points out that the birth canal is much smaller than would be "designed" when taking into account the size of an infant's head. He argues that the birth canal is shrinking as the number of Cesarean Sections (or C-sections) increases. In other words, with C-sections (as long as the woman has access to the procedure), there is no evolutionary benefit for women to have a birth canal large enough to birth a baby naturally. What would have been a debilitating problem for early humanity, a problem that would have prevented reproduction, has now become a manageable condition.

God seems to be in favor of C-sections, or at least it would be logical to conclude that he is, considering how popular they are. Why would a God make a being who has so much trouble birthing its own children? Why would he build in such a harsh punishment for women and their families who watch new mothers suffer and risk their child's life and their own? The simple answer seems to be that God did not design humans. Women's difficulty in childbirth is simply a product of breeding over time, also known as evolution, which has selected for larger head size.

The Human Mind:

The human mind is also a clear example of imperfection. In his 2008 book Kluge, Gary Marcus shows how the mind bears all of the landmarks of something that has evolved. Among the examples levied by Marcus are three interesting quirks of the human mind: priming, confirmation bias, and motivated reasoning. Each of these has a relationship with our beliefs. Marcus says, "…our human capacity for belief is haphazard, scarred by evolution and contaminated by emotions, moods, desires, goals, and simple self-interest – and surprisingly vulnerable to the idiosyncrasies of memory (Marcus 2008, 41)."

A computer has a perfect, highly organized memory. It categorizes information in a logical and easily accessible sequence which is not subject to misinterpretation or degradation. Computers assign an address for information, such as files, so it can be quickly located. Say, for instance, I place the MP3 of the song "In My Life" in a file on my computer. Having assigned it a location, I can easily go to its address. I can look under "My Music," then follow the path to "classic rock," then on to the file labeled "The Beatles," then go to the final file labeled as the album name "Rubber Soul" that contains the actual song's file. When the various subheadings are combined, an address is formed.

Human memory is founded on context. The environment surrounding an event becomes associated with the event. For example, the smell of formaldehyde is more vivid in my memories of high school biology class than the muscle groups we learned by dissecting a cat. Oddly, when I smell formaldehyde I can remember certain aspects of the classroom experience such as my lab partner, the color of the cat's fur, or the feeling of the scalpel in my hand while I did the dissection... but I cannot recall the names of the muscles that connect to the legs of the cat, one of the intended outcomes of the project.

Context-based memory is flexible and very useful for quick decision making. However, it also lacks the accuracy of computers. As Marcus puts it, "Because human memory is thoroughly driven by cues, rather than location in the brain, we can easily get confused (Marcus 2008, 23)." It is useful in a survival situation to rapidly run through all experiences involving animals with foaming mouths. Being able to accurately recount facts about rabies, such as what it does to the human body or what it looks like specifically, may take time. Having an impression or "gut instinct" about the proper reaction based on all previous experiences may be more useful than address-style information lookup in this situation.

Human minds are easily tricked by context. Gut feelings have a strong impact on our actions. It is often easier to either believe or disbelieve something without examining or recalling facts; instead, relying on impressions and the context surrounding an event. Knowing that the last time I ate in a place with bad lighting got me sick is a bit of factual information. I know the lighting had nothing to do with my illness - still the next time I ate in a similarly lit restaurant I had a strong compunction to avoid eating the chicken (in favor of a hotdog which I knew was precooked and less likely to be dangerous).

One major flaw resulting from having contextual memory is known as priming. It is a very useful quirk of human memory, especially if you are a marketer. Priming occurs when there is a repetition of a given subject. The brain is likely to process a repeating event quicker than a rarely occurring event. For example, if you hear the name Coca-Cola often your brain will process its meaning faster than the name of another brand of soda with which you are less familiar. Another trick the contextual mind performs is to link subject matters together. Associated words or concepts are joined. Therefore, if Coca-Cola gets its message across often enough, you will associate the word Coca-Cola with the word refreshing and everything that trails from that idea (Workman & Reader, 2004).

Mere impressions and gut feelings can cause more problems than solutions, and this is easily seen in the field of criminology. And, also, in religion - and the implications on religious belief are immense, mostly because parents put a lot of effort into priming their children with a positive view of their own religious convictions.

Confirmation bias and motivated reasoning are also hugely relevant for religion. The basic premise is that humans are not objective and logical creatures. We do not always make decisions or form opinions purely based on reason. Instead, our brains seek out information that will confirm, or support, the ideas we already have. (Bordens & Horowitz, 2001). If an individual is already primed to have positive associations with a particular religious view, confirmation bias allows the view, right or wrong, to be reinforced. The information they seek will most likely confirm their already held beliefs.

Motivated reasoning is a part of what helps support confirmation bias. Motivated reasoning is a fairly simple concept. People treat information more critically if it goes against their primed beliefs. Conversely, they more readily accept information that confirms their expectations. Combined with contextual memory and confirmation bias, motivated reasoning ensures that things like miracles are accepted as reality rather than viewed critically. Objective reasoning for accuracy barely figures into miracles at all. (Ratneshwar & Mick, 2005).

Perhaps it is my own confirmation bias at play, but I find the brain a "miracle" of poor planning. It works in spite of itself. If God were designing the human mind to be perfect and flawless, logic would be more prominent and information would be stored accurately and accessibly. Instead, we evolved, and natural selection favored the ability to remember more generally and make quick decisions. We are left with these highly evolved "lack-of-design" flaws that we must learn to overcome - including the flaws that allow for the creation and more importantly transmission of religious ideas.

Animals and Design (or the lack of)

To reconcile the many vestiges and flaws mentioned above one could argue that God did not design humans from a blank canvas. Instead, some creative theists claim, He created evolution and allowed it to run its course until it led to a species He favored. Although it accounts for the true age of the Earth and makes some sense for a being with infinite time on its hands, there are a couple of problems with this line of thought. First, it makes for a passive, absentee God. If setting things in motion was God's only chore in the creation of humankind, then there would be no reason to pray to him for intervention or know his will. A perfect designer would also be expected to create a perfect process and to have access to adjusting the process to remove unnecessary flaws. Evolution is not such a process. It is neither perfect nor tunable. In fact, there is a phenomenon known as "runaway evolution" where the process of evolution - which favors the ability to produce offspring over all else - can actually impede an organism's survival.

Also known as runaway sexual selection, this happens when a characteristic gets emphasized through evolution to an extreme degree. The Irish Elk is an excellent example of runaway sexual selection. The Irish Elk's absurdly large antlers became a favored characteristic of the female elk, who reproduced with those bucks that had the largest antlers and thereby steadily increased the size of the antlers until they became a deadly burden on the males (Pastor & Moen, 2004). The selection of large antlers was so out of control that bucks had to use more calcium and phosphorus to produce the horns than they could take in; which leads to weak bones and a lack of fat reserves for the winter. The species eventually went extinct as a result of the burden (Monastersky, 1999).

The Argentine Lake Duck is an example of a non-lethal runaway characteristic, but they are also an example of runaway sexual evolution. Most birds, regardless of sex, have a cloaca - a hole that serves as their anus, urethra, and reproductive orifice. Male ducks, also known as drakes, however, possess a very unique body part in the bird world - a penis. What makes this organ even more unique is the size?

The Argentine lake duck has a penis that is 20cm when flaccid, but 42.5cm long when erect - roughly the length of its body. This penis, the largest of any bird, is spiked at the base, somewhat corkscrew-shaped, and has what might be considered a "brush" at the tip (McCracken, Wilson, McCracken, & Johnson, 2001).

The Argentine Lake Duck's unique penis is the result of some amazing evolution. Another characteristic of the Argentine Lake Ducks' sex lives is that females are often unwilling participants in the sexual act. They typically struggle and attempt to get away. In response, the drakes developed spikes at the base of the tail that help them prevent females from escaping the copulation (Mayell, 2001).

To counter the continual sexual attacks of male ducks and maintain some level of sexual selection on her end, the female ducks developed a vagina that is long and corkscrew-shaped. It's so convoluted that, if the female isn't cooperating in the act, the male is not likely to fertilize her eggs. The male's convoluted penis is a way to navigate this maze-like organ, and the brush at the end of the penis is likely used to brush away the sperm of competing males.

This intense arms race of sexual adaptation seems like a very odd design decision. Why would an all-powerful, all-loving, all-knowing God create a system like this? It doesn't make sense to subject female Argentine ducks to constant "rape" or to allow something so doomed to fail as the Irish Elk. These hapless animals have a "choice," such as it is, between living and procreating. An all-powerful God would not force their perfectly designed creations to make such a horrible choice… but natural selection does.

Animals are not perfectly created. Humans are not

perfectly created. Evolution is not perfectly created. The Universe is certainly not perfectly created for us. Systems all around us are horribly inefficient and poorly designed. Shouldn't we expect God to do better? How can perfection create such imperfection? Evolution explains all the biological factors. Godless universal forces explain the Universe.

If the illogical mess of life, the Universe, and evolution were created by God, what a colossal waste of his time. Nothing is designed well. With our limited human capacity, we can imagine many improvements to ourselves and the Universe we occupy. The idea of God doesn't explain our Universe, it only makes it messier. The only way God can exist in a system this flawed would be as an absentee father who kicked off the Universe and moved on. While I would say I appreciate Him putting things in motion, I, with all my raised arrector pili, see no reason to worship him.

Chapter Three: Organized Religion's Role in Society

"Religion is an insult to human dignity. With or without it, you'd have good people doing good things and evil people doing bad things, but for good people to do bad things, it takes religion."

Steven Weinberg

"We have just enough religion to make us hate, but not enough to make us love one another."

Jonathan Swift

What is religion's role in society? Is it as a moral compass, a giver of hope or purpose, or a blueprint for how people should live?

Religion can act as a force for good or ill. I wouldn't argue that religion is completely devoid of value. There are certainly some who draw strength from their religious community, just as there are those who use it for evil. The same is true of any organized group, regardless of religious affiliation, including businesses, governments, charitable organizations, sports teams or social groups. Religions, however, claim to be more than just profit-seeking businesses or organizing forces like the government. Religion, proponents claim, is the absolute set of laws by which people should live. It claims to teach the "right" way to live and to be the arbiter of morality for its practitioners. Our expectation, then, should be that religion generally improves society and is a force for good. Religion, logically, should be held to a higher standard. Instead, I would argue that as an institution, religion tends to cause more harm than good. As a moral compass for society, religion is defunct. As an institution that brings hope to society, religion is lost.

The topic of religion's place in society has been explored more times than I care to count, but I will recount a couple of arguments with the idea of providing context. Karl Marx's "opium of the people," is a very typical view of religion in society, though the quote is out of context. Marx's point was that religion gives a reason to continue living when other reasons are difficult to find. It is the "sigh of the oppressed creature, the heart of a heartless world." Marx also said when suffering is sufficiently reduced, religion should be cast off. Religion, he explains, is nothing but the illusion of happiness and by discarding it, people can be truly happy. "The demand to give up the illusion about its condition," he said, "is the demand to give up a condition which needs illusions." In other words, if you can give up the illusion of religion, you have moved past the need for its comfort.

Epicurus believed that Gods existed as a moral compass, an ideal to be achieved. The Gods of Epicurus were disinterested in the lives of humans. They existed solely as role models. It is somewhat like what the infamous "Drake Equation" showed for extraterrestrial life: Drake's equation showed that it is almost a certainty that life outside of Earth exists, but that the idea of meeting intelligent life is irrelevant. Though there are almost certainly aliens, the chance of contact, because of the vast distances of the Universe, is basically nil. Just as one should not live life solely to meet aliens, Epicurus was saying that one should not live life only to meet the Gods.

Finally, Martin Luther believed there should be a separation between revelation and reason. He believed arguments from revelation should be left in the church and that reason should be used to conduct the business of government. If the two are mixed inappropriately the people are likely to become confused as to the difference between justice and forgiveness. His belief, ironically, leads to one of the classic arguments against a traditional Christian God. The argument goes like this: How can God be both perfectly just and perfectly merciful? The two are at odds. To be just, one must mete out a punishment that is appropriate to the crime. To be merciful, one must reduce the just punishment through compassion. To Luther, this is accomplished by the difference between the secular authority (giving justice) and religious authority (giving mercy or forgiveness).

In the coming section, I will focus on religion's role in degrading political systems and in world tragedies, two areas that are less commonly discussed.

The Rise of the Christian Evangelist:

n. e·van·gel·ism (ĭ-văn'jə-lĭz'əm) (The American Heritage Dictionary of the English Language, Fourth Edition, 2009)

1. Zealous preaching and dissemination of the gospel, as through missionary work.

2. Militant zeal for a cause.

Having been born in 1980, I find that my understanding of evangelism, and more specifically evangelicalism, is somewhat different than it might have been had I been born to an older generation. It is easy to get lost in word usage. Those that are evangelical evangelize, but not all that evangelize are evangelical. The "square" is a "rectangle," but not all rectangles are squares.

The difference is this; evangelism, or "gospeling," is synonymous with proselytizing, the active courting of potential converts, whereas Evangelicalism is a sect of Christianity that emphasizes the experience *of* conversion. Simply put evangelism is an act of recruiting, whereas an Evangelical is a type of person with a specific set of beliefs. For the sake of simplicity, I will refer to the movement as (Capital E) Evangelicalism. Though the definitions seem only subtly different, the difference is vast, especially when it comes to the nearly ubiquitous Evangelical movement in the United States.

Evangelicals have entered politics to an unprecedented degree. I think of them as Polivangs (short for Political Evangelicals). Once an undercurrent of emotional reasoning, they have now flooded the realm of rational political debate with a tsunami of irrationality. Examples of their influence abound in just about any debate over abortion, stem cell research, or so-called "family value" issues.

The 1970s saw the rise of the Polivangs as what Frank Lambert called the "Moral Majority" to combat the rise of the 1960's counterculture (Lambert, 2008). The movement focused on what they considered "Christian" concerns. They were interested in moving abortion rights, euthanasia, Israel, and what they termed "family" to the forefront of American values. Reason was washed away in favor of biblical interpretation and single-issue voting. Fiscal policy became secondary to being pro-life.

The upwelling legitimized famous Polivangs such as Tim LaHaye and Jerry Falwell and the movement gained strength in politics and mainstream culture. The election of a score of Polivangs into local and national government fueled the movement. Jimmy Carter brought Polivang ideals to the Oval Office. His born-again platform helped push him to the White House. Now, the Polivang dominance is so prevalent that one could argue it has become a requirement for office! Ronald Reagan, Bush I and II, Clinton, and Obama used their evangelical roots to appeal to their constituency. Donald Trump's relationship with the Polivang community is possibly more troubling due to its dissonance. Trump doesn't seem to be very religious, though he has been able to weaponize Polivangs for political gain. Reports from early in his presidency described a president with loosely Christian views but without attachment to a specific sect or church. He seemed to not be able to distinguish mainline Christianity from Evangelicals (Lee, 2017). Trump was aware of Polivang voting power and made a conscious choice to leverage it. Trump also seemed oblivious to scripture or liturgies. He stumbled his way through appearances at churches during his candidacy and made promises to Evangelical leaders in order to garner their support. It worked. Despite Trump's many, many non-evangelical traits, around 81% of Evangelicals voted for Trump, an unprecedented quantity (Martinez & Smith, 2016).

The Polivang movement is an unavoidable part of political life. Democrat or Republican, liberal or conservative, what was a movement to restore "traditional family values" has become a political hot-potato to such a degree that no candidate can deny belief; those who do become instantly unelectable. To be exact they would likely lose 53% of the vote for nothing more than their lack of belief, according to a 2007 Gallup poll (Jones, 2007). Atheists ranked last on Gallup's scale of electability. Hearteningly, atheists did rank above Scientologists in a 2008 Gallup poll - when asked whether they had positive, negative, or neutral views of various religious categories, atheists scored a whopping 13% positive, while the poor Scientologists came in at a pitiful 7%. I guess it is better to believe in nothing than alien DC10s dropping spirits into volcanos (or whatever madness they get up to in Scientology).

Still, Christian religious affiliation would clearly give a political candidate serious advantages. According to a different poll specifically looking at different sects of Christianity, Methodists, Baptists, Evangelicals, Catholics, and even Fundamentalist Christians all had more than 70% of respondents with either a positive or neutral opinion of the group (Methodists went as high as 96%) (Jones, Americans Have Net-Positive View of U.S. Catholics, 2008). This clearly shows a preference for Christianity is not a single party issue. The Polivangs cross party lines -they are the religious right and the religious left.

Conversely, a 2018 study performed by Lake Research Partners during the midterm elections showed that candidates who identified as "humanist" didn't suffer. The study noted that 72% of Democrats would not let a candidate identifying as atheist affect their vote. There have been notable examples (really just a couple) where atheists were able to hold their ground or, in one case, be elected. Gayle Jordan earned nearly

30% of the vote even after being attacked for her lack of belief by her opponent. Jared Huffman, an agnostic humanist, won by a landslide in consecutive elections. The overriding concern of the voters in the poll was policy positions, not religious belief. So, there is some hope. Still, atheists and other non-theists are massively underrepresented, considering we make up nearly 25% of the population, according to the Lake Research Partners poll (Bardi, J. 2018).

It's not hard to see the impact that the Polivang movement had on the generation raised knowing only its dumbed-down rhetoric and poor reasoning. The polarization is very real. Moderates on both sides (those who buy bad reasoning and those who don't) are becoming more and more rare (U.S. public becoming less religious.2015). I often hear that the divide between secularism and theism is growing and that there are relatively few people occupying the middle ground. I cannot help but agree. I see myself as a part and product of this divide.

What may be most frightening, however, is the rhetoric that has resulted from the movement and the emphasis on belief in the Bible. Republicans charge liberals with being secular and say conservatives are the party of the religious. Liberals are viewed as heathens and moral relativists who are more interested in "taxing and spending" than ethics. Many Liberals look down on the Bible-based reasoning of the religious right as bumpkinish and anti-scientific. Both of these characterizations are certainly flawed, but there may be some hidden truth in there, too.

One may ask, though, isn't the loss of logic a fair price to pay for an improved moral base? I would counter with, have we truly become more moral with Bible-based reasoning? Has moral absolutism really allowed us to avoid catastrophe? I say no. Moreover, absolutism is only absolute rhetorically. When the rubber hits the road, it seems all bets are off and everyone is a moral relativist. It's a phenomenon we have seen time and time again.

Divinely-Inspired Atrocities

It's nearly impossible to argue against faith itself. It would be a significant step forward if everyone were to admit one simple fact: *no one* knows the absolute truth of the nature of the Universe. No one can be sure that there *is* or *isn't* a God. That admission alone is enough to change the conversation. It may open the door to more evidence-based thinking and the consideration of alternatives.

Alternatives are the key to the acceptance of outside ideas. In-group and out-group thinking is at the heart of conflicts around the world. The constant fighting between Christians and Muslims and Jews and Muslims seem to be our generation's most obvious examples of how religious groups can turn people, who don't think as they do, into non-humans. If your enemy is not a person it is easier to commit destructive acts against them.

Think about it! Is it easier to shoot a person or a squirrel? Is it easier to shoot a wolf that killed your sheep or someone who is a mother or a daughter? This may seem a little harsh or even unrealistic, but then how do you explain all of the atrocities that people commit against other people who look, act, dress, or simply believe differently than them? How can events like the Holocaust be ignored? We don't need to look far to find examples of man's inhumanity to man - they exist in our grandparent's generation, our parent's generation, our own generation, and are happening right now.

Here are a few notable examples:

Rwanda-1994

Between April 7 and July 15, 1994, in Rwanda, during the turbulent end of the Rwandan civil war, the Hutu - a political and ethnic faction in the region looking to gain power - killed over 800,000 people belonging to the rival Tutsi and Twa groups. They collected names of individuals who were in the rival Tutsis and moderate individuals within their own organization who might sympathize with the Tutsi cause. The list was then used to systematically wipe out all opposition, their families, and their sympathizers. The Hutus also targeted the U.N. Peacekeeping troops, hoping that it would force a United Nations withdrawal (A brief history 1400-1994.1996; Barker, G., 2004).

So, what are the roots of this atrocity? The Tutsis and Hutus lived peacefully for hundreds of years. German and then Belgian colonists ruled the nation until they were forced out of the country in 1962. Eventually, there was a split and two countries were formed: Rwanda and Burundi. There was a struggle for power in Rwanda for decades leading up to the genocide, including a civil war that never quite resolved. The tensions between the diverse groups were high, and the allegiances of the church, far from bringing people together under the common banner of faith, did more harm than good.

The area had long been predominantly Roman Catholic (Catholicism was brought to the country by the colonists). Churches were meant to be a place of neutrality, supposedly acting as a sanctuary outside of the law. During the conflict, Tutsis sought safety and counted on the churches to provide it for them. Except, the Catholic Church favored the Hutus, and they often did not offer the traditional sanctuary and safety of the church to Tutsis. Even worse. In at least one instance in Natrama, Tutsis tried to escape the violence and hide in a local church, only to find out it was a trap. They were all killed by Hutu soldiers. In another case, a pair of nuns were actually convicted of aiding, actively, in the genocide (Rwanda nuns await genocide verdict.2001; Consolata mukangango.2016; Morgan & Samso, 2007). These nuns turned over more than seven thousand Tutsis that sought refuge in their monastery. In 2001, Consolata Mukangango (a former Mother Superior) and Julienne Mukabutera (A Benedictine Sister) were sentenced to 15 and 12 years respectively. Instead of easing tensions and providing safe-haven, the Church was an active participant in the violence.

Darfur, Sudan-2003

"Darfur."

That was all that needed to be said in the early 2000s to invoke thoughts of atrocities and destruction. With the conflict in the Darfur region of Sudan still ongoing, it has become part of daily life all around the world. What happened in Sudan that made the entire world sit up and take notice? There is some debate about how the conflict actually started, but one event certainly cemented the hostility and gave rise to the genocide that still roils in the region to this day (Copnall, 2013).

In 2003, an allied group of rebels struck a government installation. The government naturally responded in the form of aerial assaults on the rebel stronghold (Q&A: Sudan's darfur conflict.2006; Emily Wax, 2006). Back and forth fighting between the two groups led to complete unrest and the displacement of somewhere around 2 million people. The death toll estimates vary from ethnic group to group, but the smallest number I've seen published was 50,000 the largest is 500,000. Obviously, this is a rather large gap, so it can be certain that the full truth of the situation is not known. What can be known for sure is that many people died and many were left without a home.

Some argue that the government was acting through a recruited group called the "Janjaweed," a group of militiamen that were recruited from local herdsmen. The Janjaweed were said to be conducting ethnic cleansing by attacking villagers who were of the same ethnicity as the rebel factions. The government claimed that they were not involved with the Janjaweed, but the coincidence was too big to ignore.

A vast majority of the population of Darfur is Muslim. Both sides of the conflict hold similar religious beliefs. So why am I talking about Darfur in a book about Atheism? It would seem like religion had nothing to do with the fighting. And that is true to some extent. Faith was not a direct cause of the conflict in Darfur. However, it certainly did not stop the fighting. Why hasn't the faith of these people led them to resolve their conflict under the guiding hand of their God? Instead, Muslims rode into the mosques of other Muslims and demolished them.

Of course, Sudan is no stranger to inter-religious issues. The large Muslim majority frequently fight against the Christian and Animist minorities. This instability has seriously increased the likelihood of a disaster. The dictator of Sudan, Omar al-Bashir, was quoted as saying, "We will gain nothing from relinquishing the Shari'a because he who seeks people's satisfaction by causing God's indignation loses everything (Lesch, 1999)." His decisions, and the decisions of many of the people controlling the country, are informed by religion. Since religion has either failed to stop the conflict or poured gasoline on the fire, those decisions are dangerous.

Kosovo-1998

Kosovo is a land that has been fought over for centuries. On one side there are the Albanians who believe that Kosovo is their traditional homeland. They believe that they are descended from the Illyrians who have occupied the land since the Stone Age (Biberaj & Prifti, 2019). On the other side, there are the Serbians who claim the land was part of their kingdom during the middle ages (History, bloody history.1999; World: A history of tension: Serbia-kosovo relations explained.2019). When the Serbs fled Kosovo, because their land had been conquered by the Turks, they were replaced by Albanian Muslims. This tenuous situation continued into the 20th century when Serbia joined with other Balkan states and pushed the Turks out of the region. When the Serbs pushed the Turks out of Kosovo it put the Albanian Muslims, who had grown in number over the years and represented well over 80% of the population, in a difficult position. To the Albanians, the Serbian push was nothing short of an occupation.

Struggle after struggle was framed by violence, massacres, displacements, and reprisals. Finally, a new character was brought into the struggle, a man named Slobodan Milosevic. Milosevic preyed on the sentiments of the Serbs, many of whom felt as though they were being repressed by the Albanian majority. He rode the wave of Serbian nationalism all the way into the presidency of Yugoslavia. Milosevic tried to keep the failing Yugoslavian nation together as it crumbled. Croatia split off and he made war to ensure the rights of his Serbs. Bosnia left the Yugoslavian union and Milosevic drafted men from his home in Serbia to protect his ethnic brethren from what he saw as an attack by fundamental Islamists (Milosevic's yugoslavia.2014). Soon, all that was left of the former Yugoslavia was Serbia and Montenegro.

Back in Kosovo, Albanians were rising up against oppression from the Milosevic led Serbs and the Serbs were retaliating. Kosovo turned into a hotbed of aggression. Milosevic's army committed unspeakable horrors again to the Albanians. There was looting, robbing, raping, and a massive amount of killing, with bodies burnt and put into mass graves to hide their numbers. In the end, according to the United States Department of State, around 10,000 Albanians were killed and 1.5 million were forced from their homes (which represented around 90% of the Albanian population) (*Ethnic cleansing in kosovo : An accounting* 1999) (*Ethnic cleansing in kosovo : An accounting* 1999).

The religious underpinnings in the Kosovo tragedy are obvious. The Albanians are by and large Muslims and the Serbs are mostly Orthodox Christians. The struggles they have been going through for centuries are outlined by a fight of faith. It is hard to say for sure that without the religious pretext things would have been different, but there are some assumptions that we can make: Religion didn't help to stop these atrocities. There would be no need for religious tolerance if there was no religion. Muslims were destroying Christian Churches and Christians were destroying Muslim Mosques. In the end, the divide could be seen as a sort of holy war with eternity in God's good graces as the reward. Would this attitude help to moderate or lessen the violence? Why should it?

The conflict has gone on so long that it may be hard to place blame on anyone at all, so any attempt to explain it is a gross oversimplification. The history itself is fascinating and worth further examination. I encourage each reader to find their own truth about the problem. All these tragedies are a lot to take in, and if you are like many of us, you may even find yourself feeling some sense of responsibility or outrage that more was not done. On the other hand, you may be like many others and feel nothing at all in regards to these tragedies.

It comes down to who is in your in-group, and who isn't. If your in-group consists of only those people in your country, your state, your school, or your household, then it is hard to see these tragedies as things that are happening to real people. The victims are in your out-group. They are people far away, who look or believe differently and thus are not-you. Some people are more inclusive. They see their in-group as the entire world, and are compelled to act or grieve.

We hear it all the time, but we are truly the internet generation. The ability to talk to people everywhere in the world is how we turn the entire world into our in-group. We are the "Facebook" generation and we can build communities with anyone, anywhere. We are also a fact-hungry group. With a simple glance at our phones, we can look up and learn about anything and anyone. We can opt to be informed. With information, we realize that we aren't so certain we are right about our beliefs and faith, and the borders become blurred. The entire world is accessible to us, and we can make a difference.

Failed Expectations

In Rwanda, the Tutsi had an expectation, a trust that the clergy they looked up to, would act in their best interest. Maybe they believed this because they knew these people as friends or at least acquaintances, but what is more likely, is that they felt this way because they believed the clergy were people "of God." Their intentions should have been entirely pure, especially faced with the prospect of eternal damnation. They *should* have forsaken their own lives to save those of the people around them, and their reward would be heaven everlasting. Obviously, it did not happen that way.

No matter how often the religious fail to live up to the ideal of their religion people don't discount the religion. The people of Rwanda rebounded and are now becoming more religious than ever! Their faith is so unflappable they could watch as people who were part of their church's hierarchy, who had literally sentenced thousands of their countrymen to death, return to the Church. Their mentality is borderline Stockholm syndrome!

The pattern of expectation and let down permeates the Catholic Church and many other Christian branches. The examples are all over the news. We hear about them on a daily basis. A preacher sexually assaults an altar boy. A minister misappropriated funds from the collection plate into private gains. A pastor sleeps with one of his parishioner's wives. These are all things that are familiar to our society. We write these acts off as the acts of sick individuals. Why don't we look at this as a problem with religion? What is the belief in God bringing to the table?

The most common argument is "morality," but clearly, belief has not improved these people's "moral fiber." If anything, the church has given reprehensible individuals an organized structure within which to operate. Many studies have been performed that attempt to correlate religion and corruption and have had varying results. Recognizing the variability, an additional study was conducted and published in The Journal of Business Inquiry in 2013. The study found there was no relationship between religion and corruption. That may seem contrary to my thesis, but take a step back and think. Corruption is a sin. So, shouldn't there be a difference?

Man is fallible, but the church is supposed to be infallible. When there are more religious adherents in a region, whether Christian or Muslim, shouldn't there be less corruption? People are people, they act the same regardless of their beliefs. Maybe religion is a neutral force, not outright acting as a force for ill, but it certainly isn't acting as a force for good (Shadabi 2013).

A common question asked by atheists is: if God is all-powerful and all-knowing, then why would he allow Man to be fallible in the first place? Why would he allow genocide, if he has the power to stop it? Theists argue that God is either acting for the greater good by allowing evil, or that he shouldn't be held to human standards of good and evil. In the first argument, God allows evil either to test humans or to prevent the greater evil of removing human free will. This infers God is not capable of allowing free will and preventing genocide. Theists love to put limits on their God. The second argument makes God so separate from man as to certainly make humans not built in his image. A God who doesn't share our human moral compass certainly couldn't have given us moral commandments by which we should live. After all, he doesn't have a human's standard of good and evil. He has an ancient Greek God, humans are cattle, world view.

I am actually addressing two separate questions here. The first is the question of religions' role in the minds of those who are directly involved in the conflicts. The other issue is the role of God in creating and preventing these conflicts. Where is his, for lack of a better word, responsibility?

The religious response to this is often, as put by Stanley Fish, "if Adam and Eve were faithful because they were programmed to be so, then the act of obedience (had they performed it) would not in any sense have been theirs. For what they do or don't do to be meaningful, it must be free (Fish, Stanley 2007)." This argument is flawed for one very simple reason. It is assumptive.

Conceptually, to be divine, God must be above the understanding of humankind. Rational human argument is, therefore, nearly impossible. Falling back on "the Lord works in mysterious ways" is a common way conversation about the validity of religion breaks down. It is used as a defense by the religious when they have to explain why God would do something they don't understand. Obviously, theists recognize they cannot understand how God works, but when they make arguments such as Fish's, they ignore their lack of understanding. Fish is assuming God's intent (if he could be said to have intent) is to have people make all their decisions on their own.

Why? Why would God want that? The argument breaks down instantly since the intentions of God are unattainable by man. Fish's argument is that God wants a true tribute to his greatness, but why would God want or need a tribute? The argument is nonsensical. You cannot engage in a debate if you choose to end the conversation with a response that is nothing more than saying "because." Why does God allow evil to persist? Because. Why did God want Adam and Eve to have free will?

Because.

Herein lies the great religious debate. Atheists require more than "because" as an answer. We want an explanation and reason. We are the same people who question everything, as irritating as that can be. We are not, by definition, able to accept things on face value. We are scientists who question, with continuously reducing detail, how everything works. A theist is likely to see a car run and say, "that vehicle will be useful to get from here to there." Whereas an atheist is likely to see the car and say, "Sure, the car can get us from here to there, but how does the engine work?"

I feel the need to fight for the future of my children, whose prospects for true intellectual achievement are in danger because of this struggle. I am not comfortable in a world where their education is stunted because there are people that believe evolution is "just a theory," clearly not knowing what theory means in this context. I do not want them to have to learn that the Earth may be only 6,000 years old because one book says so when there is a plethora of resources that show otherwise. The push to Bible-based reasoning stands to destroy the reasoning so ingeniously created thousands of years ago by ancient logicians who focused on logical arguments and reasoned debate.

Not to say that all theists choose to be ignorant. That is not the intention. Instead, I am saying that atheists question everything, whereas theists are likely to seek out information in some areas, but feel that some things are better left not understood. The choice to be ignorant must necessarily lead to a temperament of ideology. If you choose to not look too deeply into evidence of how man was created, then you have not earned the right to force your "ideas" on others.

Chapter Four: Science and the Soul

"I think I am, therefore, I am... I think."

George Carlin

"...the famous philosopher Descartes ripped body loose from mind and turned the very soul into a ghost that haunts its own house."

Walker Percy, Love in the Ruins

Where Are We in Eternity? A Discussion of Heaven and the Soul

We think of eternal life after death as something akin to our current mode of existence; our existence just continues along the same trajectory, but forever. Immortality or eternal life after death runs into two major issues, the mechanism, and conceptual incongruence. We don't know how it could happen and we can't comprehend what eternity is, either in terms of joy or pain. Our mind is literally not built to comprehend its infiniteness. Many people spend their lives striving to reach their version of a perfect "eternity," but few have plumbed the depths of what eternity would really mean.

And yet, eternal life after death is tantalizing. Life is so vibrant that it's hard to imagine it ending. To paraphrase Christopher Hitchens, life is a bit like a party. The trouble with dying is you have to leave the party while everyone else keeps on partying. You are missing out on the good times! So what if that party never ended? Attempting to comprehend the concept of immortality tests the limits of the human mind, but heaven solves that problem. It's much easier to cope with life-ending when the end is really just another beginning and everyone you liked (if they were good enough) will be reunited with you in the new life. Sure you have to leave the party, but you're going to another party. A better party, one that lasts forever. It is everyone else who is missing out!

But what exactly does heaven mean? When you get into the details of heaven and eternal life in paradise, things start to get tricky. Imagine for example an eternity of riding your favorite roller coaster or listening to your favorite song. A common conception seems to be that heaven represents an eternity of joy, but we cannot even decide what makes us happy in the moment. How could we possibly describe what would be joyful for eternity?

In John Milton's Paradise Lost, Satan discusses his plight with one of his fellow fallen angels; Beelzebub. Recently kicked out of heaven, he is now the master of hell. Satan makes a few points that are extremely cogent: "The mind is its own place, and in itself can make a Heaven of Hell, a Hell of Heaven (Milton, 1667)." As long as Satan has the free will to define his own version of happiness, he declares, he would rather "reign in Hell, than serve in Heaven." If heaven and hell are, as Milton describes them, in one's own mind then the conception of heaven as a static place of eternal joy and hell as a place of eternal pain are logically untenable.

This chapter is about atheism and the soul. So, why does a discussion of eternity matter in a chapter about the soul? Eternity is an infinite stretch of time, but the soul is a very different concept - a metaphysical object or substance that makes us unique and has apparent value to Gods and Devils. How can the two ideas be related?

Well, they are, intimately. Simply put, the soul serves as a "gateway" to eternity. If no eternity exists, what is the need for a soul? If no soul exists, then how does one reach eternity? Consider that everything physical in the known universe disappears or disintegrates over time. In order to achieve eternity as a human "presence," we would need something more resilient than our physical stuff, hence, a soul. This is the classic philosophical debate between physicalism and dualism. Physicalists believe the world is just the world. It is made only of the physical world we experience. The dualists hold that humans are two entities, the physical (our bodies) and the immaterial (our souls) and they exist separately. If the body dies that then leaves open the possibility that the soul doesn't join it. Put differently, the soul is the mechanism through which eternity and an afterlife can be achieved.

A common argument for the existence of a soul is our ability to argue and feel. No physical object we know of has the capability of feeling emotions. After all, as far as we know, rocks don't feel joy, cows don't cry, and grass doesn't feel love. Our body is an undeniably physical object, incapable of feeling. The soul, an intangible force, must, therefore, be how we feel our emotions, not the corporeal body, which must be just a mere vessel for the soul. I would argue this view should be restated. Instead one should say, "*I don't understand* how a physical object can feel emotions." because it's akin to saying, "I don't understand how it could work that way, and therefore it must not." Imagine how it would sound, to modern ears, if someone said, "I don't see how germs can cause illness, therefore it must be evil spirits." The argument is weak and ignores modern neuroscience.

Another argument commonly posed says, because we are beings with free-will, we must have souls. The argument goes like this:

1. All physical objects are subject to a world where outcomes can be determined (i.e. drop a rock and it will hit the ground, or better the laws of physics say that force is equal to mass times acceleration. So, we can determine the force if we know the mass and acceleration). This is known as determinism.

2. Deterministic systems don't have free-will

3. Humans have free will

4. Therefore, humans are not just physical objects.

The assumptions in an argument like this are hard to confirm. Can a deterministic system "look" like free will? It seems likely that a system as complicated as the human mind could produce what seems like free-will. So, do Humans have free will? Here we are back at the idea of irreducible complexity, and we arrive at the same conclusion as before - it is possible for complex systems to arise without being designed. I look at many things in nature, the Grand Canyon or a snowflake for example, and contemplate how something so complex could arise naturally. Even though it seems extremely unlikely that either could arise without some intercession from an outside party, there is always an explanation. My own ignorance creates the illusion of complexity. Because of the vast complexity of the interaction of our minds with the world, the illusion of free will *could* exist. Not "I think therefore I am," but "I cannot think of it therefore it is not." One could call the confounding of our minds and the wonder it produces a numinous state, a state of awe or mystery.

Numinous thinking is not only the realm of the religious. Christopher Hitchens often pointed out there should be a separation between the numinous feelings we all experience and a connection with the divine. One can be awed without religion, I often have been when looking at the night sky and simply thinking about how small humans are in relation to the vastness of the Universe. In those moments it is as if the Universe is collapsing in around me. There is a weight to it, an almost physical sensation. Is that God's presence? Am I sensing the incredible power of Gods or spirits? Is my soul resonating with the awesome energy of some external force? No, it is just a numinous moment. My limited human brain has trouble processing the vastness of space, the intricacy of a snowflake, the grandeur of the Grand Canyon. In those moments, I am overcome with wonder and awe, and these things all seem as they would *have* to be divine in origin. But, as an educated, modern human, I know each phenomenon can be explained by natural laws, a work of nature, not of God.

The argument for free will, as stated earlier, is an argument based on ignorance. It says, "I can't fathom how a physical (natural) system could produce something that looks like free-will, therefore there must be something else; a soul." What if the system is simply extremely, to the point of being indescribably, complicated? If we were able to perfectly understand every aspect of the human brain and the environment affecting it, then we might be able to predict the decisions it would make. We just currently lack the resources to model a system that complex. There is certainly precedent for this determinism in modern neuroscience. Phenomena such as priming, where outside, seemingly unrelated, events can cause a significant change in behavior, hint at the underlying predictability and the amazing complexity of the human mind as discussed in Chapter 3. In a 2007 article for the New Yorker Magazine on how hot and cold coffee affect emotional responses, Carey Benedict noted:

> "New studies have found that people tidy up more thoroughly when there's a faint tang of cleaning liquid in the air; they become more competitive if there's a briefcase in sight, or more cooperative if they glimpse words like "dependable" and "support" — all without being aware of the change, or what prompted it (Carey, 2007)"

What about the rest of the natural world? Are there things in the natural world that have (or seem to have) free will? The Heisenberg uncertainty principle highlights one such example. Heisenberg showed that we cannot "determine" both the speed and position of particles. The particles are physical objects, but we cannot determine certain aspects of their existence. In other words, they are indeterminate. This is not to say we are simply lacking the technology to measure the speed and the position, but rather that it is impossible to see both factors. The best we can do is apply probabilities to make guesses about the missing variable. We can say that 50% of the time the particle's position will be in a certain range, but we cannot say *why* it is there. It seems like the particle can decide where it wants to be or how fast it wants to go. It is not subject to determinism.

Does the underlying indeterminism of a particle mean particles have souls? I certainly would say no. Just because I cannot determine both the position and speed of the particle doesn't mean that the particle has a soul. It follows that just because I cannot determine with 100% accuracy the actions of humans doesn't mean they have souls either - and humans are far more predictable than a coin flip.

How Much Does Your Soul Weigh? A Problem of Mechanism

Consider all the things we've been able to measure through technology. We can see a match light on the moon. We can weigh subatomic particles. We can even estimate the weight of the entire Universe! Yet, with all of this technology, we cannot conceptualize a process to measure the soul. Why is the soul so removed from inquiry?

There are many who would argue the soul is so incorporeal that it cannot be measured in an empirical way. The most compelling argument I've heard for avoiding empiricism was the argument of causation. The causation argument says all actions have causes and thereby all actions we take are the result of the causes which preceded them. In some sense, free will is lost in the process. Imagine you could understand all causes in an effort to explain why you chose the Cinnamon Toast Crunch cereal rather than eating a bowl of fruit. You would find many things influence your buying decision like human evolution, upbringing, your taste buds, the marketing efforts of the cereal brand, and many many more. If you were able to predict all causes, you could predict the effect. From a theistic point of view, arguing against causation makes sense. God would have to be the first cause in the Universe, but also the idea of free-will would be degraded. I personally cherish the idea of my own free-will and therefore the argument from causation rings a little hollow.

Sometimes I think we would be better off not knowing we are nothing but the result of cause and effect. If we are truly a product of the causations of the world around us, then we are not responsible for our actions. No soul, no free-will, no purpose, no responsibility. How could one punish a murderer for killing if his actions were not his choice? Without free will, the murderer was fatalistically drawn to kill. The answer is that punishment is simply another bit of causation to add to the mix intended to prevent further crimes from the murderer, and from other people thinking of murder. Punishment is meant as either a deterrent and/or preventative. The murder is "caused" to go prison and, because of his new location, he won't be able to kill anyone in the general public. Eventually, he will recognize that killing caused his prison time and associate the act with his negative experience as a captive. In the future, he will be less likely to kill. In addition, it "causes" other people to reconsider homicide. The argument from causation does not mean the human brain does not work. The brain is still a decision-making engine and everything we do feeds it data for review. The data we take in from experience, and thereby causation feeds the system. There is no need for any incorporeal or external force.

As Owen Flanagan noted, the idea of God infected human society with the need for free will, but there is no need for free will when you have voluntary action. As long as an external entity is not forcing us to act, we are free. The idea of God led to the idea of heaven and free will was needed as a way to filter those who belong in heaven from those who do not. Without free will, it would be just luck or predetermination which leads to the high or the low road, an idea that many would consider unacceptable. If there was no heaven and hell, there would be no need for free will.

Causation is a primary concern of science, which may explain why many people fear science. Causation seems to short circuit the idea of free will, but in truth, it supports the idea that we have control of our own fate. In a way, we are all doing science, every moment of our day. We react to the world that we are experiencing through experimentation and learning. The world around us can only be understood by means of our science, though the method is usually rudimentary and subconscious. Humans are hardwired for a cycle of experience, inference, and retrospection. We touch a hot stove, burn our hand, realize that if a stove is turned on it is likely hot. We then look back to the original event as a marker of what may happen next time the stove touching opportunity presents itself. This may be rudimentary, but it is nonetheless science. Owen Flanagan put it like this:

> "Jesus, Buddha, Confucius, Socrates, and Aristotle make their recommendations based to some (possibly large) degree on empirical observation. They are, insofar as they are engaged in cognitively respectable ethics, doing what I earlier called ethics as human ecology. Lives lived according to the ideals they propose go better, indeed are better, than lives lived according to the statistical norms. How could they know this? Observe people who live both ways and see who flourishes. Water your plants. They will do better than if you don't. Eat Breakfast. You will feel and think better than if you don't...I see no interesting difference between the recommendations of the great

ethicists for how best to live than those of architects for how best to build bridges or aqueducts. Both are based on empirical observation relative to certain considered end goals (Flanagan 2002, 70-71)."

Every inference we make is based upon the scientific (causation) method even those that are religious. The difference is direct versus indirect experience. A religious person often believes based on the experience or inferences of others (Mooney, 2012). This is important for progress. An individual or society cannot progress unless it gains from the collective inference and experience of its people. Where the system often goes awry is in the retrospective stage (formalized in science as the process of peer review).

Reviewing or reflecting on experience helps to frame our learning. Formalizing this process is important, otherwise, we may arrive at incorrect conclusions. It would be a mistake to infer you should always step on the gas when a traffic light turns yellow just from watching cars speeding through a light. In fact, it would be an extremely dangerous practice and you might be more likely to get into an accident than to your destination! Instead, during retrospection, one should consider all the information available to them. If the experience (observation) about cars speeding up is combined with the knowledge that many accidents are caused by this practice, we arrive at a very different conclusion. First one may understand that it is likely not wise to speed up when the light turns yellow and it is better to be cautious. A better policy comes to mind: removing your foot from the gas at a yellow light and hovering over the break. Reflecting rationally allows for correction to knee jerk inferences.

If the scientific process happens in our minds with every new observation or experience and allows us to navigate a changing world, then let's use it to try to understand the soul. To do so, we must first have a clear definition of the soul. For our purposes, the soul is the part of a human that conveys the essence of themselves. Further, this part is separable from the physical body and thus is available to pass on to an afterlife. For a soul to be relevant to humans it has to contain the essence of who they are - their thoughts, memories, and personality. It cannot simply be an animating energy that allows a physical being to move. Something about the person must be conveyed beyond the flesh; something that is beyond the process of consumption or decay that converts mass to energy. I say this because I have often heard the argument that something about us is conveyed upon death as we decompose or are consumed by nature. The idea is that there is a constant cycle and since energy cannot be created or destroyed, we take part in the system when we die. And, though this is true, it has no bearing on the idea of the soul because the soul must also be conscious. Having no consciousness during one's "life after death" negates the value of an afterlife as it is the complete dissolution of the self. What is the value of an afterlife in which we cannot actively participate or even be aware? What is there to look forward to in life after death if you truly cannot experience it through the lens of yourself, and how could a soul be punished or rewarded in the afterlife if it is no longer the collection of self that performed actions on Earth? To punish the tabula rasa would be cruel. Thus, the soul must be conscious and aware of itself. There must, in other words, be a sense of self.

The self is a tricky thing to define and is often interchangeable with the idea of the soul. Probably the best description of self that I have heard is one related to a

Radiolab interview with neuropsychologist Paul Broks where he described the self as an introspective narrative of our life. Broks says, "The extended self, which is what we normally think of when we think about ourselves, is really a story. It's the story of what's happened to that body over time (Abumrad, J. and Horne, E. 2007)." In his estimation, we all cling to a story of our lives based on our experiences, memories, the world around us and our expectations for the future. When asked who we are, we relate themes based on this story. This internal narrative is (as far as we know) what sets us apart from animals and is fragile. A blow to the head can erase the story completely.

Our attachment to the soul and to the idea of an afterlife is a desire to not let our story end. The soul stands in for our sense of self. It becomes those characteristics of our mind that make up who we are. The soul becomes an amalgamation of our attributes including our memories, our experiences, our "story" or even our genetics. In order to have an afterlife, this amalgamation must be conveyed after death to have any value, likely even including genetics somehow, a purely physical trait. If you are open to the idea that the theoretical soul has a physical component, then the possibility of measurement is opened. Here we enter the realm of science - and science has indeed tried to quantify the soul.

The Science (and Medicine) of the Soul

The concept of the soul *is* open to scientific inquiry. Scientists have actually explored the concept using traditional scientific methods. As early as 1907, a scientist named Duncan MacDougall attempted to weigh the soul. The goal of the study was to determine if he could measure the soul as it left the body at the moment of death. The first step in the study was to find patients who were near death in order to be present at the exact moment of death (as it was defined at that time). MacDougall took the beds of the terminal patients and placed them on a large scale when he thought they were nearing death. He would periodically weigh the patients and then, once they passed away, weigh them again post mortem to see if there was a difference. His published results became known as the 21 grams experiment, for reasons that should be obvious: MacDougall believed he had evidence that there was a measurable decrease in human weight, 21 grams, that could be attributable to the soul leaving the body. MacDougall's results were dubious and have been widely criticized for a variety of reasons. Most obvious among them is his tiny sample size - Out of six terminally ill people measured, his conclusion was based on only one case. Two of the six were discarded for measurement errors, one lost and regained weight, and two more patients lost weight at death but the loss continued for some time. For several of the patients, the actual time of death might have also been unknown, since determining the moment of death was difficult with the limited technology of the time. For the same reason, MacDougall would not have been able to measure changes in weight with any degree of precision, and whatever weight change he might have seen was easily attributed to other biological processes. A lot, after all, happens after death (Mikkelson 2003.)

MacDougall was persistent, however. He also measured a group of dogs in the same way in order to show dogs don't have souls. He felt he confirmed his 21-gram "result," though no one has been able to repeat and confirm his experiments since.

Even over 200 years ago, MacDougall's experiment was

considered dubious at best and yet it still seeds conversation about the soul. He still has his defenders and detractors! People still propose experiments based on his work, though experimentation is minimal outside of fringe organizations. Why the gap in study? This can best be understood through the same lens as the problem with praying to regrow a limb. People don't really expect God to help an amputee regrow an arm and so they don't really pray for it. People don't really think a soul could be detected as it leaves the body, so they don't conduct experiments to find it, even as they pay lip service to the idea.

A search for the soul may benefit from studies that examine changes in personality resulting from brain injuries. Brain injury studies examine the soul indirectly, as the soul is synonymous with the mind and resides in the brain. When the brain is damaged, the mind is changed, and the soul is altered. Possibly to an extent where the person owning the brain/mind/soul is unrecognizable. There seems to be a clear link between traumatic brain injuries (TBI) and violence and criminal behavior. Young people who have suffered a TBI tend to have increased risk for drug and alcohol addiction and suicide (Williams et al., 2018). Their tendencies may represent massive departures from their normal "self."

Think about what you cherish about being yourself; maybe your intelligence, your memories, your love of music, your sense of humor, or your compassion for others. A well-placed blow can reverse any of these. If I can hit you in the head and change you enough, in what sense is your "you" more than just your brain? Are you still you if you no longer have the same characteristics or memories which make you uniquely you?

One popular example of traumatic brain damage is

Phineas Gage. In 1848, Phineas Gage was working on the railroad when an explosion propelled a 43-inch long tamping iron through his face and brain. Doctors were able to remove the iron and Gage recovered, though he was never the same. Gage was very different after the accident. His friends said he wasn't Gage anymore (Twomey, 2010). A passage from his doctor highlights the change well:

> "His contractors, who regarded him as the most efficient and capable foreman in their employ previous to his injury, considered the change in his mind so marked that they could not give him his place again. The equilibrium or balance, so to speak, between his intellectual faculties and animal propensities, seems to have been destroyed. He is fitful, irreverent, indulging at times in the grossest profanity (which was not previously his custom), manifesting but little deference for his fellows, impatient of restraint or advice when it conflicts with his desires, at times pertinaciously obstinate, yet capricious and vacillating, devising many plans of future operation, which are no sooner arranged than they are abandoned in turn for others appearing more feasible. A child in his intellectual capacity and manifestations, he has the animal passions of a strong man. Previous to his injury, though untrained in the schools, he possessed a well-balanced mind, and was looked upon by those who knew him as a shrewd, smart business man, very energetic and persistent in executing all his plans of operation. In this regard his mind was radically changed, so decidedly that his friends and acquaintances said he was "no longer Gage (Abumrad & Horne, 2007)."

So, was Gage still Gage? Was his soul intact? If Gage

prided himself on his steadfast work ethic, good manners, and good business acumen, then clearly all the ways he used to identify himself were gone after his accident. Was his soul damaged in a measurable way when the tamping iron removed part of his brain? If so, then his brain is indistinguishable from his soul, which raises a new question: When he died in 1860 after a hard day of plowing, would it be the new Gage or the old Gage who is judged in preparation for the afterlife? Would it be the pre-damage Gage or the post-damage Gage, who passes on to heaven or hell?

In a 21st century example, actor and comedian Tiffany Haddish spoke out publicly about her complicated relationship with her mother. Her mother was in a bad car accident where she was thrown through the windshield, suffering a severe head injury. She survived, but after the accident, Tiffany's mother became violent, abusive and unpredictable. Eventually, Tiffany and her siblings had to be removed from their formerly happy home. Her mother's behavior had changed to such an extent that Tiffany has said it was like she was possessed. Someone else was in there, but it wasn't her mother. To Tiffany, her mother was as good as gone - all because of a brain injury (Fernandez, 2019; Jeffries, 2017).

I struggle with the idea that the Gage and Haddish's mother, after their accidents, were likely not the type of people who make it to heaven. The pre-accident versions of Gage and Hiddish's mother would be, and would get dragged along with their alter egos to hell. It is incredibly arbitrary and capricious, and more than a little cruel, to think that a person could live perfectly and morally for half of their lives, have a terrible accident, and end up in hell because of a change to their brain which was completely beyond their control.

Modifying the brain to produce changes in personality or behavior has been in practice for a very long time. Even before people knew the causes of disease, people drilled holes in skulls to expand the mind and help the sick. In the middle ages, they called it trepanation. The practice can be found in cultures throughout the world. These holes were not fatal, skulls with trepanation holes have been found with evidence of years of healing. Back when sickness was thought to be the work of demons or spirits, trepanning was thought to release the evil from the skull and may have had the added benefit of relieving pressure from brain swelling. Whether it has an effect on the mind is debatable, and it is obviously no longer a part of common medical practice, though some people in the '70s attempted to use it to alter their consciousness, much like a psychedelic drug (Horgan 2015).

More recently, in the 1930s and '40s, Portuguese neurologist Antonio Egas Moniz became renowned for going past the skull and cutting into the brain to change it. It was a literal hacking of the brain's structure. This practice, known as psychosurgery, was a fad around the world in the early part of the twentieth century. Dr. Moniz won a Nobel Prize for his work in psychosurgery in 1949 (if you have a moment, google him and see if you think his picture seems exactly like the type of person who would enjoy cutting into brains). His particular specialization was leucotomy, or what we now call lobotomy. The process involved removing or altering the connections in the brain surgically in order to change behavior.

Walter Freeman modified Moniz's process and helped mainstream lobotomies. He even lobotomized John F. Kennedy's sister Rosemary (very unsuccessfully). Freeman believed the thalamus was the seat of emotion and wanted to disconnect the thalamus from the frontal lobe in order to change the behavior of mentally ill patients. Freeman was an evangelist for his procedure. Around 50,000 lobotomies were performed between 1949 and 1952. Freemen performed around 3,500 lobotomies personally over the course of his career, even performing lobotomies on children as young as 4 years old ("Frequently Asked Questions About Lobotomies," 2005). The idea of a healthy person undergoing a lobotomy should be abhorrent as we know they would cease to be themselves. Imagine being aware you are about to undergo a procedure that could alter the way you view the world so profoundly as to make you unrecognizable (emotionally) to those who know you best. It would be the same as losing yourself altogether and could be seen as a type of homicide. Indeed, after being lobotomized many of Freeman's patients changed dramatically, they began to act childlike and have poor impulse control. He created new challenges within his patients while trying to solve the original issue, and the patients were never the same again (Harlow, 1868). Thorazine, a medication, eventually replaced physical lobotomies but was no less potent in its effects on the brain.

One must ask what happened to these unfortunate people after death. If the brain is the mind, and the mind is the soul, is it the lobotomized or pre-lobotomized version of the soul that gets transmitted to the afterlife? I can think of two outcomes, assuming that the person in question is religious and adhered (as best they could, given their age and abilities) to the tenants of their religion. If the genuine soul is the person post-lobotomy, then they start with a blank slate upon healing from their surgery. Their pre-lobotomy sins would be forgiven, and only their post-lobotomy actions, heavily influenced by their brain damage, would "count" towards the afterlife. If the pre-lobotomy patient has the genuine soul, any post lobotomy repentance would be meaningless and their sins would forever be on their metaphorical record. But then, what happens to a four-year-old lobotomy victim?

But how about something more subtle? What we put into our bodies can have a significant effect on our personalities and mental state. Legal and common "drugs" are a big part of this: Coffee makes you more awake. Alcohol reduces inhibitions. Ritalin gives focus. There are countless examples of chemical brain manipulation through prescription and self-medication - we can change both the chemical and physical structures of our minds. While more temporary than psychosurgery, the lessons are the same. Altering an individual's mind changes them, sometimes permanently and more importantly it calls into question what it means to be "me."

Our experiences are also constantly shaping who "we" are. Lewis Carroll once famously said, "I can't go back to yesterday -because I was a different person then." Events shape our brains and personality. Every new experience makes me a new person. I am literally not who I was when I was younger (which is probably a good thing), or who I was when I typed the previous chapter of this book. Is my soul the same soul, then? Am I the same me?

Today, electricity and magnetism are being used to alter human brain activity. In 2017, researchers published an article in the journal Nature Human Behavior where magnets were used to alter mood. That is, altering human brain activity without surgery or added chemicals using only electricity and magnetism When magnetism was applied to the dorsolateral prefrontal cortex, scientists were able to alter people's perceived value of certain songs. They were able to make the listener find them more or less valuable by deadening or stimulating neurons. The researchers saw this as an early step to alter the brain's "reward circuitry," which can drive behaviors like overeating or depression (Medrano, 2017). Researchers have also been able to motivate patients by passing electric currents through the anterior midcingulate cortex. The patients with the applied current felt more determined. The patients said the feeling was mostly positive (Sample, 2013). Personally, I love music. I can't imagine changing my love for music. I might even feel like I would not be me if my taste and love of music were changed or taken away. Both of the example studies changed the fundamental nature of the people in them, but that is only the tip of the iceberg. There are changes in the brain which have a much more profound impact on the minds they house and thus, on the soul. How much deeper can we go?

Deeper Down the Rabbit Hole

Radiolab, a podcast that explores science about big subjects, did an amazing episode on the self. It was called "Who Am I?" I recall it being the first time I thought about how mutable the self really is. They relate a story where a woman "loses" her mother due to an aneurysm. An aneurysm is a spontaneous bleed in the brain that causes brain damage due to a combination of oxygen deprivation and irritation of the brain tissue by the blood. Aneurysms are life-threatening, but even after her mother was healthy and had healed, the damage remained. As a result, the woman she had known all her life seemed to be gone, replaced by another personality. This new mother was more carefree, less inhibited, and even had different likes, dislikes, and interests. In the interview, the daughter relates:

"The mother I grew up with died that day and was replaced by an entirely different person, who just happens to have the same memories and body and family and address as my dead mother (Abumrad & Horne, 2007)." A change in the mother's brain changed who she was completely. It must mean her "self" was her brain. There is no other reasonable explanation.

When I think of the story, I wrestle trying to find an explanation for the soul in her story. Which version of her mother would pass on to the afterlife? The mother was happy with her new self and was presumably happy as her old self. Both are equally "right" yet entirely different. Which soul is the "right" one? I can't see a way to rationalize a path that would make sense. The theist might, I imagine, respond along the lines of, "God would know which was right and chose that one," but what if the change in her personality made her a criminal or sinner? Does she deserve to be damned eternally? What if the opposite was the case, a criminal changed personality after a blow to the head, an aneurysm, or a stroke? What if this new personality repented for his past actions, and then got hit by a bus? If he was "fixed" by brain trauma, he shouldn't really go to hell. Then again, does he really deserve heaven after the life he lived? Does brain trauma create two souls? What a mess!

Alzheimer's, dementia, and a variety of other well known (typically) end-of-life diseases cause dramatic changes in the personalities and sense of self of their sufferers. We know these conditions are a product of illness in the mind, with a combination of physical, chemical, and structural changes in the brain. The version of me that has Alzheimer's is arguably not myself. After a whole life lived as a certain version of me, it would, therefore, be wrong to assign an eternal punishment or reward for my actions during dementia. If a patient with

Alzheimer's shouldn't be judged based on decisions made while ill, should someone with schizophrenia or chronic depression be judged for their actions? Illness is illness, and this point can be taken all the way down the slippery slope to the extreme.

If brain chemistry is known to change the "self" and we are all products of this chemistry, a loving God would never punish us for behavior that is simply the result of a chemical imbalance or damage to the brain. If so much of our decision making is caused by factors out of our control, then free will ceases to be a factor. The nature versus nurture debate becomes the only factor. Palm Computing founder-turned-neuroscientist Jeff Hawkins once said, "We are our brains. My brain is talking to your brain; our bodies are hanging along for the ride."

We are, in essence, a collection of memories. Damage to the physical structures of the body (specifically the brain) can cause the loss of part or all of these memories. The clear link between mind/soul and body means, even if we can imagine it to be possible, that the mind cannot exist without the body. My memories would not be able to survive the death of my brain. If my memories cannot pass with me at death (a dead brain) then what is a soul? Without the essence of what I am ascending to heaven with me, my soul has no value. Any reward or punishment is being given to the wrong entity. Viewed through a logical lens, the typical religious image of the soul is nonsense.

Chapter Five: Religion in Business

> "All religion, my friend, is simply evolved out of fraud, fear, greed, imagination, and poetry."
>
> *Edgar Allan Poe*

> "When I started out in the franchise business, I didn't know exactly what I was doing by promising God his part if he helped make my enterprise a success, but I now think that that is the reason for my success ever since."
>
> *Colonel Sanders*

The histories of religion and economics are intertwined. It has been this way since the earliest civilizations. It may not be completely obvious why this would matter in a book discussing my personal brand of atheism. Indeed, it can be hard to see how the Church acting like a business is a refutation for the existence of God. Church, in this context, represents a house of worship or organized religious group of any sect. While it's true religion and business are not mutually exclusive, I would say that the reason it matters to an atheist is straightforward: Religions, as we know them today, have been built, shaped, and maintained, and corrupted by the influence of money.

The intermingling of business and church has changed the tenets of religion as the powerful and wealthy use their influence to maintain control. God/Gods and the traditions surrounding them as we know them today, might have been entirely different without the influence of money. Religion cannot be an accurate depiction of the Universe if it is not free from the influences of money and power, and so organized religion becomes suspect along with God. If we can't trust organized religion then we cannot trust a God who allowed his/her religion to be corrupted. If we can't trust organized religion, then the way to heaven is not revealed to us and religion cannot offer true or reliable guidance for how we should live or pray.

We could very easily find examples of the hand of business in religion at any point in human history. 4,000 years, however, is far enough into the past and takes us to the long and storied history of Ancient Egypt. It is hard to separate the state and its power from that of the Church in early religion (or in this case, the priesthood). Ancient Egypt is a good example, Pharaohs were the chief priests and controlled the priestly class. In doing so they controlled the resources and wealth of the empire. The Egyptian priests were paid out of the offerings given to their temples. In the early priesthood, becoming a priest meant access to economic stability. As time went on, the priestly positions became social positions where individuals with enough means could purchase a priesthood. The priestly class controlled temple knowledge which included books about religion, but also medicine and science (Priests in Ancient Egypt, n.d.).

Those in power began doing the things that powerful people always do: They started changing the rules to suit themselves. For example, the Pharaoh exempted the priesthood from taxes, which put them above the common people whose offerings created the wealth of the priestly class (Mark, n.d.). The information asymmetry between the priests and the Populus was exploited through the use of religious imagery, myths, and rituals where the priests interpreted the will of the Gods and predicted whether the year's floods would produce feast or famine. Using their information advantages, such as access to information about the cycles of the Nile, the priests elevated themselves. The priests also had access to books about medicine and herbs. They brokered all of their privileged information for their own benefit. (Denning, 2014).

The priests of Delphi in ancient Greece are another good example of money and power corrupting religion. The priests acted as a direct conduit to the Gods. Specifically, the Oracle of Delphi or Pythia was in charge of prophesying the will of Apollo. The oracle may have received her visions from fumes rising from the volcano-fed hot springs, or from burned seizure-inducing herbs. In either case, consulting the Oracle was standard practice in ancient Greece for important decisions, and the consultation typically came at the price of a donation. Larger donations garnered special treatment or ease of access to the Oracle (Goodman & Maggio, 2008). The Oracle was able to guide and shape political events across the ancient Greek world.

In his writings, Herodotus mentions the Oracle's abuse of their power. For example, the Oracle urged the Spartans to attack the Pisistratidae after the Oracle was bribed by a rival faction. The Spartans attacked and drove the Pisistratidae from Athens leaving their rivals in control. Herodotus also suggested that the Oracle was bribed into favoring Xerxes and the Persians against Leonidas. You might recognize the story, as it was partially recounted in the movie "300" (2006) (Fairbanks 1906).

Christianity is no different than the ancient Greek and Egyptian religions. Examples of corruption by money or power abound in Christianity's history, making it unlikely to be the "one true" church. I hesitate to bring up example after example drawn from two millennia, hundreds of sects, and across several continents. It would be too much like beating a dead horse. Instead, here are a few well-known and particularly egregious examples: namely, televangelism, the Inquisition, the Schism, Christmas, megachurches, and interference in the Church by Roman emperors, to name a few. For more examples, watch TV most nights or do a quick google search. In the literature, I found *An History of Corruptions of Christianity* to be very interesting. Though the book's focus isn't on how money and power have corrupted the Church, it does talk about the gradual drift away from traditional Christian values. The book's relevance to the Founding Fathers of America is particularly fascinating ("An History of the Corruptions of Christianity : in two volumes : Priestley, Joseph, 1733-1804 : Free Download, Borrow, and Streaming : Internet Archive," n.d.)

I will get into further detail for some of these examples, but I want to discuss papal indulgences first, a particularly interesting phenomenon. Indulgences are absolutions granted to sinners by the Catholic priesthood, essentially purchasing forgiveness for your sins. Indulgences are still given today. The granting of indulgences is clearly corrupted by money.

Catechism 1471 allows for indulgences which are intended to remove, "...either part or all of the temporal punishment due to sin ("Catechism of the Catholic Church - IntraText," n.d.)." Ideally, this means that the church will direct parishioners seeking forgiveness to do good acts for their community. In return, the scales will be balanced and the sinner may avoid purgatory or punishment in the afterlife. It's a lot like the idea of Karma, but the benefits are wholly controlled and directed by the Catholic Church. Not all sins are eligible for indulgence, for example, if you stole something, confessed and asked for indulgence, the church may grant you an indulgence if you worked at a soup kitchen for a while. Its "community service for the Lord," and not a bad idea in itself.

However, around the time of the Crusades, it all went wrong. The Catholic Church began selling indulgences for money. The path by which indulgences went from penance to payments is actually very easy to follow. First, the Church offered crusaders indulgences as an incentive to fight in the Crusades. Since fighting in the Crusades was a form of serving God, even dying in his name, Crusaders were immediately absolved of minor sins upon death. However, some people couldn't fight in the Crusades, but they wanted to contribute to the holy efforts. Wars, including the Crusades, are expensive affairs and, in response, the Church decided that contributing monetarily to the cause was equally worthy of indulgence. The link between indulgences and fundraising was complete. This connection lingered for centuries, and Church coffers filled from the sales of indulgences ((Hulsman, 2018); Vitello, 2009). Forget doing the right thing in your everyday life, you could easily cough up a few bucks and not have to worry about it. It basically sanctioned bad behavior. One could purchase a path to heaven and feel free to sin.

It is no wonder that the sale of indulgences was a major thorn in the side of church reformationists like Martin Luther. Today, "You cannot buy one — the church outlawed the sale of indulgences in 1567 — but charitable contributions, combined with other acts, can help you earn one (Vitello, 2009)."

In the interests of fairness, I wanted to also include an exploration of corruption in Judaism. However, I could not find clear examples that didn't seem either motivated by historical biases or rely on easily corruptible religious texts as the main source of information. For example, there is a historical bias against Jews for "slaying the prophets wrongfully (4/155), taking usury and devouring people's wealth by false pretenses (Husseini, 1956)." While "usury" and "taking wealth" seems like clear corruption, the source material, and the historical context matters. For example, in the middle ages Jews had few career choices as they were not allowed into guilds. The limited job options led many Jews to go into banking and money lending (Jensen, 2016). The quotes are taken from an interpretation of the Quran. In general, there seems to be a lack of reliable ancient sources for corruption. However, a possible modern example of corruption does spring to mind:

In 2009, authorities arrested a small group of Rabbis in Brooklyn, New York, and a variety of other people, in connection with black market organ trafficking and money laundering (U.S. Attorney's Office, 2012). The Rabbis served a key role in the scam by moving money through their synagogue's non-profit charities as a donation. They would then kick back a 10% fee to the con man, a clear example of money laundering. Their scam lasted for years. The Rabbis admitted to knowing they were laundering money that was gained from illegal activity, one of which was convincing vulnerable Israelis to donate one of their kidneys for $10,000.

The kidneys would later be sold in America for more than $100,000 each. (Halbfinger, 2009)

Even if this is the only reliable example, it still illustrates my point: no religion is immune to corruption. From the earliest religions to the most modern, all religions are vulnerable to the influence of power and money. The similarities between religion and political office highlights that religion is just another system of social organization, like any other.

Again, this may not seem like a refutation for the existence of God, but it is on a couple of levels. First there is the classic Epicurean argument discussed earlier: Recall that Epicurious' argument has three facets:

- If God is capable of preventing evil deads and chooses not to, then he isn't a "good" God.

- If God can't prevent evil, then in what sense is he a God?

- If God can prevent evil and wants to prevent evil, then why do bad things still happen?

Church corruption follows this pattern. If God can prevent corruption in his churches and the clergy who serve them and chooses not to, he can't be benevolent. If he can't, then how is God worthy of worship?

Ultimately, corruption exists in all forms of religion. If God were real, then his chosen church should stick out like a sore thumb. We would know it as the church that has never been corrupted by money and influence, and favor it. Darwinian natural selection would have made it the only church worth following and all others would have fallen by the wayside. A common argument against this position is that, "we don't understand God's plan," which is ultimately another way of saying, "I can't make heads or tails of it either and I need out of this conversation in a hurry or my core beliefs might be challenged."

Let's say we accept that people are corruptible and God doesn't want to intervene on behalf of his church. Let us assume that God's rationale for this is that He wants all of his people to have free will and make their own mistakes. Now we have a fundamental problem that may not be a direct refutation for the existence of Gods, but choosing the right religion would have to be impossible. There is a classic Pascal's Wager issue.

Blaise Pascal, in the mid-1600s, argued that everyone (atheists as well) should live as if God exists because the costs of being wrong are nil and the reward immense. In other words, if you believe in God and you are wrong there is no eternal consequence, but if you are right there is an eternal reward. Pascal's Wager falls apart in one very key way: It cannot speak to which religion is the "right" religion to follow.

The real wager we all make is that our chosen religious views are the right ones. How does a Christian really know their religion is correct or if it is Hinduism or even animism? It isn't a binary choice. We all pick our ponies and hope we finish the race first.

We know churches are corrupted all the time and all throughout history. Our religious texts have been handed down for generations. The interpretation of those texts from language to language has been done by corruptible humans.

Choices have been made about what belongs in the books and what doesn't by fallible men, vulnerable to the influence of corruption. Important religious figures recognize as much: Sheikh Mohammed Abdu wrote, "It is not proper that the belief in God should be taken from the words of the prophets nor from the revealed Book, because it is unreasonable to believe in a Book revealed by God unless one already believes in the existence of God (Husseini, 1956)." In other words, you shouldn't use the books as a way to believe in God as your belief in God would have to predate your belief in the revealed - and fallible - texts.

Ironically it seems that the vast majority of religious adherents (at least in America) do not even read their religious texts. A 2017 LifeWay study showed only 20% of Christians in America have read the Bible in its entirety even though the average household has three Bibles. That means the Bible and its interpretation is left to the clergy, and we have seen where that leads ("LifeWay Research: Americans Are Fond of the Bible, Don't Actually Read It," 2017) . To add to the irony, atheists tend to have more religious knowledge than most religious people, Mormons and Jews come in a close second and third ("U.S. Religious Knowledge Survey," 2010).

Ultimately, we can't ever be certain we are living the way God would want us to live. We have no sense of what God's intention could be when it's been filtered through layer after layer of human corruption and the degrading influence of money and power. God's preferred church isn't obvious and God's teachings are likely lost. We have to use tools beyond God to understand how to be good. We clearly don't need God to be good people, and ultimately, few people actually use God as their barometer.

So why, then, do people still give money to the church?

Businesses as Churches, and Churches as Businesses

Churches are businesses. A business is defined as an entity that provides a product or service to a customer for a payment. The product or service churches provide is access to God and the payment is the collection plate. The Church acts as a distributor of access to God either directly or by acting as a guide. The parishioners act as customers and are willing to pay for the service because they don't think they could find their way to God (heaven) without the official help of the Church.

The cynical side of me says that much of Church-going is not about access to God, but rather to a "country club." The churchgoing are looking for an exclusive group of "better" people in which, for a small fee, they can belong. In that respect, I have to admit to being jealous. Atheists, as a group, often talk about the lack of an organized community where we can find a social network of people to support us through our paths in life. I will acknowledge the sense of support and community that churches provide has real value, well worth paying for. The need to belong to an in-group and put others in an out-group is a very common and very human characteristic. You can see it everywhere: football fans, book club participants, crossfitters, and churchgoers are all looking for a way to assuage their social needs. They have all sought out (and found) a community within which to connect to like-minded people. It is honestly a very nice thing, but where it all goes awry is when dogma enters the equation. Ideally, the out-groups are treated humanely, but that is not always the case (think soccer hooligans, the Salem witch trials, or anti-muslim or antisemitic sentiment). When money and the influence of people in power mix with dogma, it can corrupt the entire religion - and the community it provides - turning it into an engine of destruction.

So, let's follow the money.

Many churches require payments from their parishioners, some suggest, and some use strong-arm tactics to ensure payment. The Mormon Church, or the "Church of Latter-Day Saints" seems to have a "gym membership-like" approach to making money. According to a Reuters article, the 14 million LDS church members are expected to tithe 10% of their income to the church though less than half attend services on a weekly basis. The LDS church brings in $7 billion each year in tithes and owns more than just churches. They own malls, farms, and other commercial real estate totaling around $35 billion dollars in assets (U.S. Attorney's Office, 2012).

The LDS Church owns assets around the world that are estimated to be worth significantly more than $40 billion, especially considering their stock holdings alone exceed $30 billion ("Bloomberg - Are you a robot?," n.d.; Larry D. Curtis, 2018). According to a 2016 Huffington post article, church assets may be $1 trillion (Karger, 2016). In addition, their annual income has been calculated at around $45 billion. Their income and assets come from tithes but also from a variety of business ventures. Many of these ventures are not related to spirituality, either, they include TV and radio stations, farms, residential buildings, and even insurance companies (Winter, Burton, & Nick Tamasi And Anita Kumar Bloomberg Businessweek, n.d.) The LDS church rewards success with prestige - the ultimate country club.

Add a very mobile sales force of young devoted

missionaries who travel around the world to recruit new clients to the LDS, strong asset positions, and solid revenue performance and you have something strongly resembling a business empire. There is no doubt some of the funds go to good causes, but still you would be hard-pressed to find an organization that is more businesslike and open about it. The Mormon Church also has a leg up on regular business because they pay no taxes because they are a religious institution. Despite not paying taxes, the church uses its money to influence politics, such as the LDS church's well-known lobby against California's Proposition 8, a gay marriage amendment, in 2008 (Gaimani, 2004).

The Mormon church is an easy target, but it is not distinctly different from Evangelical, Catholic, or even Muslim institutions around the world. Muslim countries, in the Middle East in particular, have the good fortune of having huge gas and oil reserves. These valuable natural resources have transformed the way they interact with the world, and how leaders in these countries interact with their people. The economics of heavy oil-producing nations, like Saudi Arabia, seem to be a liberalizing force within these highly religious countries. There are open conversations about women's rights, trademark law, education, even business operating hours, as Saudis seek to join the modern economic world. While the changes within Saudi Arabia (and other Muslim countries) are promising from a human rights and global citizenship perspective, ultimately the liberalization represents a challenge to centuries of religious tradition. The decisions about what should change and how the changes should be made are ultimately made by the country's leaders which include a religious authority that holds a lot of power. The religious leadership participates in deciding whether or not downloading music illegally is against the Islamic religious law, among other things. (Slackman, 2007). The petro-politics of the Muslim world are altering the religious views of its leaders and citizens. Dogma is either washed away in the wake of the influence of money and information or twisted to fit a changing world. It is the slow degradation of religious ideals toward a universal truth. In an Article from 1956, Ishaq Husseini wrote, "The modern Muslim thinkers find in the principles of Islam a flexibility which allows them to explain and interpret with the greatest freedom while still keeping the faith intact (Husseini, 1956)."

The process of reinterpretation is standard practice for Muslim clergy. It is referred to as "Ijtihad," which translates to "free interpretation." The Mujtahid, those who are qualified to use ijtihad, are free to interpret ambiguous sections of Muslim law and that interpretation is translated to the adherents of their particular sect of Islam. There are different sects, Sunni or Shi'i for example, who accept different interpretations. Through this process, over time, the faith is changed to meet the needs of the culture and Muslim society. The Muslim faith, therefore, is flexible and has a mechanism to accept change and modernize. (Husseini, 1956). Changing, adapting, evolving in the context of faith are all euphemistic words for degradation of the core of the faith. If humans are changing religions all the time, then in what sense can a believer trust what they believe today to be the revealed "truth?"

According to a study conducted by the Religious Freedom and Business foundation, "religion annually contributes about $1.2 trillion dollars of socio-economic value to the United States economy (Hendrson, 2012)." The religious contributions in the U.S. are so large they eclipse the economies of almost every country in the world. If U.S.

Churches were their own country, they would be the world's 15th-largest economy. Churches around the world have all of the key characteristics of businesses, they hire and fire people, they purchase goods and services from other businesses, they invest and they go bankrupt.

The schools operated by Churches are a great example of their business machine. The teaching operations of religious institutions are a major element in our educational system in the United States. They employ 420,000 full-time teachers who teach 4.5 million students each year, ensuring their message is passed along to the next generation in a continuous cycle (Grim, 2017). They are a business, and they sell spirituality.

Religious Ideals in Business

Churches act like businesses and businesses sometimes, in turn, act like churches. Businesses have acted like churches for a long time, sometimes even using church-inspired or church-like dogma and cults of personality to enforce or encourage "proper" behavior. We are becoming more aware of how religious beliefs are impacting our business structures. As a result, we're seeing a growing awareness of "moral character" that is fueling today's social battles over businesses making choices about who to serve or how to treat employees based on religion. For example, Religious adherents are outspoken about their right to run their businesses in a way which matches their dogma, and they bristle at the idea of other businesses using a different moral compass. Imagine two hypothetical businesses:

The first, run by Christians, who ask their employees to sign a contract agreeing to follow Christian principles. They also require employees to say a daily morning prayer, praising God together as a group. The second company requires employees to follow traditional Muslim beliefs where female employees of all faiths are required to wear a headscarf. People in the second company are granted breaks and space to perform their multiple daily prayers praising Allah. In the United States, both are free to do so as long as they avoid being discriminatory in who they hire. However, also in America, where Christianity is one of the dominant religions, the Christian business leaders would feel justified in stirring up an outcry against the second business, despite them being equal in restrictions. Neither business can thrive without customers and the truth of America is there are enough people looking for Christian run institutions to keep them open and rarely enough to support businesses founded on other faiths or no faith.

Both of these hypothetical companies are also using the incentive of money (in the form of jobs or favor from the people in charge) to push their beliefs onto their employees. In reality, this can be more blatant than even our hypothetical scenarios and, in fact, it often is. There are companies all across the United States, selling everything from groceries to gun sights, whose leaders interlock their faith and their business (and many aren't Churches) (Nisen, 2016).

Hobby Lobby, for example, is founded on religious ideas. David Green, Hobby Lobby's founder said, "It is by God's grace and provision that Hobby Lobby has endured. Therefore, we seek to honor God by operating the company in a manner consistent with biblical principles." Green is an evangelical biblical literalist. Using Hobby Lobby resources, he helped take a case to the Supreme Court where he won his company the right to refuse to provide female employees with birth control as a part of their health care coverage - all because he and his family felt it may risk ending a human life (Withnall, 2014). Green also famously used company resources to purchase biblical artifacts, some of which were smuggled illegally into the United States (Barajas, 2018).

The Hobby Lobby case highlights a bevy of issues that arise when businesses try to be churches. Does America's separation of church and state extend to business decisions made in the name of religion? Also, at play is the identity of the organization. Is Hobby Lobby a religious institution or is it simply a for-profit institution run by religious people? If another company were to purchase Hobby Lobby from the Green family, would the religious identity move with it to the new organization or could Hobby Lobby become a Jewish, Muslim or atheist company based on their new ownership? The line is ever-moving. Even small changes to the religious beliefs of the organization's Christian nature (think sectarian differences) could change the company entirely. The slippery slope comes when an organization claims exemptions to state or federal laws because of their religion. There would be nothing stopping companies from claiming a new religion that doesn't believe in offering prescription drugs or hospital care to their employees (think Christian Scientists) or other basic services. Cynically, it's easy to see how a profit motive would encourage a company to use a religious loophole to save money by altering or decreasing employee benefits (Brennan-Marquez, 2014).

When the Hobby Lobby case reached the Supreme Court of the United States, the outcome was less than positive. The Supreme Court ruled in favor of Hobby Lobby and struck down the provision of the Affordable Care Act (ACA) that required companies to have insurance for employees which included birth control. The Obama administration then reworked the law to give women working for companies like Hobby Lobby access to birth control through the government when their employer declines. While women ultimately kept access to birth control the Supreme Court decision set a frightening precedent (Newton-Small, 2016).

Hobby Lobby isn't alone. Chick-fil-A founder Truett Cathy once said, "As Christians, we have an obligation and responsibility to abide by the principles of the Bible." He backed up his biblical literalism by coming out publicly against a variety of referenda intended to give equal rights to LGBT citizens (O'Connor, 2014). The non-profit arm of Chick-fil-A also contributed millions to anti-LGBT causes (Horovitz, 2014). While the Cathy family's position has moderated over the years, they did use (and likely continue to use) their resources to attempt to effect political change that matches their religion-based view of the world.

There are a host of businesses around the United States, bolstered by a 2018 court ruling, who deny service to members of the LGBT community. The news blossoms with refusals to sell flowers or cakes to gay couples. Denial of service is not so far from racial segregation, a true blight on American history. How is denying service to someone because they are gay any different than denying them service because they are black? Unmarried heterosexual couples, especially the women, are also discriminated against - in Arizona, Arkansas, Georgia, Idaho, Mississippi, and South Dakota it is legal to refuse to sell contraceptives based on moral grounds (Barker, A., 2015). I assume there are parts of the country where I would be denied service because I am an atheist (if they found out). All that is needed for rampant prejudice to creep in is for regular citizens to stand by and let a sense of "other" be sanctioned.

The sense of "other," the creation of outgroups, is not new. It has been part of both religion and economics for a long time and can be seen in the union of the two (Karimi, CNN Design: Allie Schmitz, Matthews, & CNN, 2018).

Religion and Economics

Religion begins as individuals holding their own beliefs. Eventually, seeking commonality or efficiency, people band together and start to make shared "truths" from their beliefs. From that initial organization, a church is created. The church would gain power and find ways to grow. It would have to survive in a competitive marketplace - angling for adherents and finding a niche to fill which sets its brand apart. Like any business, this natural progression follows basic economic theory.

Economic theory and religion have gone hand in hand for a long time. Sometimes, economics have been blatantly used as a way for theists to describe the superiority of their own religious group. For example, the Protestant work ethic was used as a justification for religious discrimination for decades. To early Calvinists, economic success was an indicator of God's favor. If they worked hard and amassed wealth it was because they were God's chosen people and clearly destined for heaven. Max Weber (1905) famously said Protestantism was the cause of the industrial revolution and the rise of capitalism, but this ignores contributions made by people of all faiths (and those with no faith) from all over the world. The idea that Protestants work harder, save their money better, and are more successful smacks of eugenics.

Either way, religion and economics are intertwined. As discussed earlier, money has influenced religion, but religion has also influenced money. Not through the divine hand of God, but through the social norms, the religious faithful impose upon themselves. According to a 2013 study, Protestants take the loss of a job more seriously than the general public. Tellingly, those who live near Protestants feel the same serious loss. The impact on non-protestant neighbors highlights the cultural norm rather than their religious superiority. The study highlighted a 40% increase in suffering among the Protestants and Protestant-adjacent people. They derive their sense of worth from their jobs (Luzer 2013). Apart from Protestants, religion seems to impact wealth through its support for education and the modern push for school, then marriage, then children (Keister 2011).

Religion is a social force and, like all social forces, those who participate in the movement set themselves apart from those outside. The example of the Protestant work ethic highlights how creating expectations within a group can affect group outcomes. The pressure of the group keeps adherents working harder and saving more, a pressure which persists.

The economics of religion is now an entire field of study. Adam Smith, economist, author of *The Wealth of Nations,* and father of the classical free-market theory of economics, viewed religion in economic terms noting the differences between state-controlled religion and countries which allowed for religious competition. Smith pointed out that when competition in religion was permitted (a free market of religion) religious variety thrived. He was also a critic of ruling religions perpetuating a system which prevented the improvement in conditions of the lower classes.

Max Weber continued with Smith's ideas in "The Protestant Ethic and the Spirit of Capitalism" where he emphasized a rational choice model for religion. To Weber, religions were just choices or brands, and consumers had options between those choices. If they didn't like the tenants of one religion, they could choose another to follow - and they did. In his theory, changes in religious attendance across the world were really just the result of brand preference. Protestants, who Weber saw as special, had a hard work ethic and received additional benefits and therefore the religion grew in a sort of Darwinian selection of Protestantism. This has come to be known as the "Gospel of Wealth." Adding the threat of heaven or hell into the mix represents the penultimate cost or benefit and has the additional power to change the decisions of someone who truly believes.

In contrast to Weber's utilitarian theory, the modern behavioral economics movement is embracing religions' lack of rational choice. Behavioral economics recognizes humans as non-rational people who are not necessarily concerned with utility. Instead, this theory states, humans are more interested in right and wrong, fairness and equity. Religious beliefs affect an individual's decisions and, as such, are the purview of economics. (Bateman 2011).

A combination of both utilitarian rationality and behavioral economics' more emotion-driven decision making makes sense when looked at through the lens of modern economic theory. Here, religion is seen as a consumer good. In a 2011 article, Parteek Goorha explored religion as a product.

As a primer, economics breaks "goods" down into four categories: private, common-pool, club and public. The difference between the types of goods is a function of how easily a person can access the good without paying (its excludability) and the likelihood the good can be used by more than one person (how rivalrous the good is). Religion is traditionally seen as a "public good" because it is easily accessed by people who don't pay and it can be used by many people without diminishing the experience of any individual.

Goorha argues religion is, in fact, a "club good." The main features of club goods are higher excludability but low rivalry. In other words, it can be used by a lot of people, but not without paying. Not paying for a good is often referred to as freeriding. Freeriding at Churches is limited through social pressure and frequently more direct means. Publically giving during a service is a way for group pressure to be applied to all participants in a service. Churches, such as the Mormon church, require a regular tithe from their parishioners and freeriding is strongly discouraged.

Religion may be seen as rivalrous as well: The value of the church experience for each member of a church or religious organization is diminished as more participate in a religion. Members are less involved in ceremonies as the congregation grows. They also have less contact with leaders and have less access to church roles that provide status and social standing to members. The rivalry, or loss of exclusivity, among parishioners, is a real consequence of the growth of churches. When the church grows large enough, there are more people in the church with the same number of church leaders - which means a decrease in access. Goorha also points out that trust could be seen as a main "product" of religious affiliation. Catholics are likely to believe that other Catholics are trustworthy as they share a common set of beliefs, but as the Church grows it admits people who are less trustworthy to its ranks. This degradation of trust decreases the value the Church provides, in this way the church becomes a private good.

Religion may have a positive economic impact. In a study

published in 2013, a group of researchers found a correlation between religious attendance and feelings of well-being during socio-economic change. In their study, they looked at Polish citizens during the formative years of "career-building". There was a clear correlation between religiosity and coping with work uncertainty. People who attended church more frequently reported feeling less depressed when work was uncertain - up to a point. When work uncertainty was rated as "very high," the group's ability to cope leveled out. Religion acted as a buffer against mild to moderate work challenges, but the buffer went away when financial uncertainty peaked (Lechner et al 2013).

Beyond giving adherents a common ground for trust-building and a social network that can be used to weather hard times, religion seems to have had a hand in building the economic world within which we all live today. There have been quite a few studies which argue the rigid social hierarchy of Catholicism reinforced the feudal system. It wasn't until the growth of Protestantism, with its greater egalitarianism, that capitalism proliferated. Religion has even been credited with providing the foundational social capital needed to permit democracy.

Businesses around the world can learn a lot from the church model. One notable organization that acts a lot like a church is Crossfit. Crossfit is a large entity but local franchises build a family within that particular gym much like the Catholic Church is a large central organization, but the family is built at the local Church level. The model has worked extremely well for both the Church and Crossfit.

Another interesting way economics can explain religion is the creation and growth of religious sects. In economics, the downfall of large organizations is the issue of free-riders in the system. The larger the group the harder it is for the group to prevent free-riders. A natural solution to the problem is to reduce the size of the organization. Religion has adapted a clever way of taking the best of both large and small organizations. A religious person can be a Christian and, as a subset, be a Baptist. By doing so, they can be part of the larger religious order and connect with the larger group, but also benefit from the smaller group, the sect. Within the sect, the individuals benefit from the smaller group. They benefit from greater participation within the group, have better cooperation with other members, and are able to prevent free-riders. Groups can be made even smaller by getting down to the church level. It's even been argued that Protestantism led the way to capitalism through its proliferation of sects! The increasing number of sects produced increasing connections, the argument goes, and as a result, a greater number of financial and commercial transactions could occur. Also, splitting away from the Catholic Church allowed the smaller sects to innovate in a process much like evolution on isolated islands (Clark 1951).

You can see the market forces at work in the creation and collapse of churches. They grow, the attendees lose some of the benefits because of the increased scale and new sects are formed. Those sects either grow or are consolidated with other sects and the cycle repeats. Interestingly, there was a growth in sects through the 1960s, think of this as the growth phase of a new business sector. Then in the 80s, the "sector" started to decline. Think of the decline as the industry consolidation phase of the business sector. Some churches die out as the industry consolidates.

A side effect of smaller group size is the ability of the group to self-police. Churches can set their agenda and rely on the smaller group to maintain their expectations, where a larger group cannot. "Strict demands strengthen a church in three ways: (i) they raise overall levels of commitment, (ii) increase average rates of participation, and (iii) enhance the net benefits of membership (Karacuka 2018)."

Does it matter if religion is more of a club or private good or if the growth and changes in religion can be explained through economics? Of course it does. If the religion were true, it shouldn't act within the parameters set out by rational economic theory. It shouldn't work the same way a gym or social club does. And yet we see the consumers of religion follow economic laws, changing behavior in predictable ways as their religions grow in size, resulting in a decline in church attendance. Economic patterns describe religions better (based on the evidence of church choice and attendance) than does the idea that there is a church/religion that is offering the one "truth" to all people. As it stands now, it is far too easy to explain religion in terms of economics and that diminishes the likelihood of it being an ultimate truth. Human nature is at religion's core, instead of something "otherworldly."

Chapter Six: Replace My Dad with God

> "The Lord is like a father to his children, tender and compassionate to those who fear him."
>
> *Psalm 103:13*

> "I would say that the hardest thing about being a parent is these goddamned kids."
>
> *Andy Richter*

Humans are social creatures, and Religion is a societal meme, passed between members of a society down the generations. As an atheist, I find its transmission interesting but also supportive of my lack of faith. In general, when things can be explained by natural or regularly occurring causes it degrades the need for God. The need for God is eroded. In this case, I can explain religious belief as one of many ideas transmitted across cultures and time - it is a societal meme like any other, without any divine providence behind it. In this chapter, I will review how it is passed down and across. I will also review some of the psychological underpinnings of religion, from before Sigmund Freud to modern thinkers.

Religion can be passed on in a variety of ways. Family, social circles, societal pressure, self-discovery and personal aspiration all play a part. These ways of transmission are not equal and, of all of these methods, the religious beliefs of one's immediate family - especially one's parents - have the greatest effect.

Our Parents and Religion

Parents are likely the most responsible for the religious beliefs of their children, and their teachings carry the most weight. This is no surprise - we trust our parents and there is a biological imperative for parents to care for their children. Trusting our parents is a basic survival necessity. We all start helpless, with no ability to fend for ourselves. We remain in this state for many years, gradually lessening the burden we place on our parents as we mature and gain abilities during our march towards adulthood. In the meantime, though, parents help us when we are most vulnerable and weak. They teach us how to comprehend this complex world and, if we are lucky, they even take us to Little League. The human species would have disappeared a long time ago if parents didn't look after their children, and if children didn't trust their parents. Babies are just a little too tasty to the predators of the world to survive on their own. After all, babies are the other, other white meat (thank you Fat Bastard).

The programming that helps us trust our parents makes survival much easier. Thanks to natural selection, it is difficult to break the blind trust in parental authority. A consequence of this built-in trust is children will absorb the traits of their parents, which includes all types of beliefs. Sports team affiliations, educational preferences, political beliefs, how to prepare a hotdog correctly (mustard, not ketchup of course), and religion are all passed from parent to child. I have been attempting to de-program my children for years and I am happy to report, as they approach teenagers, they trust nearly nothing of what I tell them. Job well done - except for the hot dogs. They do those correctly.

The power of a parent's influence on religion was recognized by early Muslim communities. Some Islamic sects believed that "...every man is born into the 'natural religion' of Islam, and only upbringing by his parents converts him to another religion (Gaimani 2004)." While I disagree with their specifics, it is easy to see that, consciously or unconsciously, parents inculcate their children with their beliefs. Parents use many tactics, and, according to a variety of studies, some of these are incredibly effective and are often used together for the greatest effect.

In a study conducted in 1999, researchers identified the keys to passing along religious information between parents and children (Okagaki, Hammond, & Seamon, 1999). The researchers focused on 5 key insights.

1. Children's *perception* of their parents' belief is more predictive of the child's belief than the parents' actual beliefs. No matter how fervently their parents may hold a belief, if the child doesn't have a good relationship with their parents (they often disagree or the child sees the parents as too authoritarian), they are less likely to believe the same thing.

2. Kids are more likely to adopt their parents' beliefs if they think it is important to their parents.

3. Parents who openly share their beliefs, and are open about wanting their children to have the same beliefs, pass along their beliefs more effectively. A parent who repeatedly states and explains their

beliefs (such as Jar-Jar is abhorrent because he is a racist caricature and an unnecessary distraction from the plot), and why they feel their child should share the belief (racism is wrong), is more likely to pass on their beliefs.

4. When both parents have similar beliefs, their children are more likely to believe what the parents believe (for example, that Jar-Jar-Binks is a blight upon the Star Wars Franchise.)

5. Children who have a "warm" relationship with their parents, and who see themselves as "securely attached" to their parents tend to desire to adopt their parent's beliefs. If your child feels that you love them, they will believe the way you do (and Jar-Jar is shunned!)

The first idea to unpack here is the idea that parents' beliefs and the child's perceptions of those beliefs may differ. When they differ, the child is most likely to believe what they perceive to be their parents' beliefs. Belief is not so much passed down to the next generation but altered in a sort of evolution. You can see how religion can change from generation to generation simply through the process of misunderstood beliefs being transmitted from parents to the child. From an atheist's perspective, or at least from my perspective, this shows a lack of consistency in the interpretation of the words of God. If the chain of beliefs can be altered so easily, how can anyone really believe that there's only one right way to believe? Parents seeking to prevent misinterpretation and the altering of belief, must be very clear about what their beliefs are as they pass them along to their children.

Unpacking the second and third key insights together makes sense. It is purposeful indoctrination when a parent tells their children what to believe and that it's important that they believe. In other words, parents are telling their children what they should believe rather than allowing the children to draw their own conclusions. This requires stifling a child's ability to make decisions on their own. Worse, it tells the child's developing mind that they risk losing parental love and support by making decisions on their own. I don't know if this comes from insecurity within the parents wherein they feel unsure about what they should believe and so become reliant on authority to guide them, instead of using their cognitive abilities. There is always the possibility that parents are carrying out a tradition passed down to them from their parents and they believe that tradition is more important than the value of allowing their children the freedom to make decisions on their own.

Having known a few people who have had religion pushed upon them as children, I believe it comes more from a need for security than a lack of trust. Still, the idea that authority should be accepted for the sake of authority rather than the capacity for free thought is something that atheists like myself find disturbing. It is like saying the children are never going to be capable of making an intelligent decision on their own, therefore I must tell them exactly what they should believe.

As one of a pair of atheist parents, we share a relatively monolithic view of the lack of a God. However, we are exceedingly open with our children about finding their own path. The study outlined above, however, points out that our beliefs are still very likely to transmit. It is less about a parent's willingness to allow the children to explore, then about consistency and clarity in the way parents present their religious beliefs. Parents who carry the same beliefs were found to be significantly more likely to pass these beliefs onto their children, and less likely to have those beliefs questioned. The researcher found that when parents held different beliefs children were, in turn, more varied in their beliefs - diversity encouraged the children to find their own paths, instead of following in their parents' footsteps.

The final item on the list shouldn't be terribly surprising. Children who find their parents off-putting are less likely to have positive associations with their belief system. Okagaki et al (1999) said, "The degree to which adolescents saw their parents as being authoritarian, using harsher discipline techniques (e.g., embarrassing the adolescent in front of others, belittling the adolescent), and being less accepting and nurturing was positively related to distance from conservative religious beliefs." This happens frequently, especially around adolescence: I've heard from atheists raised in strict Christian households who admit the first time they challenged their Christian belief system was in response to the weaknesses and failings of their parents. Of course, the opposite is also true - warm and loving parents are likely to be seen as ideal parents to their children, and their beliefs (and behavior patterns) are more likely to be mirrored (Okagaki et al., 1999).

I would like to believe we are good parents, but there is a good chance we have successfully indoctrinated our children with our brand of atheism. Ultimately, I believe the atheist mindset is significantly better than the religious mindset, as it teaches my children to challenge authority and make rational moral decisions on their own. However, as an atheist, I must ask myself: is it as tyrannical to force my children to believe my non-religious ideals? Richard Dawkins said that he considered the forced learning of religion by children to be a form of child abuse (Dawkins, 2015). I can understand

Dawkins' point of view and I'm self-aware enough to understand that I might be doing the same with my children. This is a good segue to classical psychological theory regarding religion and parents.

Sigmund Freud had multiple theories making up his canon of work, but two, in particular, are of interest for the acquisition of religious beliefs. Freud's Projection Theory states that religious beliefs are "Illusions, fulfillments of the oldest, strongest and most urgent wishes of mankind (Freud, 1927)." As children, we are constantly in danger and we recognize our protection from that danger comes through our parents; specifically, according to Freud, from our fathers. The love of our paternal parent protects us from the dangers of the world around us. However, as we age, the world becomes more complicated and the protection our fathers provide becomes insufficient. As a consequence, we need to find a replacement. We project our need for a father as the ultimate Father, God. In Freud's opinion, we have created Gods who act like men because the men we thought were Gods (our fathers) turned out to be ordinary men.

Projection Theory seems to explain the anthropomorphic nature of God in the Old Testament; a God who walks on the ground with man, who loses track of the people he created, and who gets angry and vengeful. He is a God who is patterned after mortal men (and not the other way around).

Freud thought that human beings want to believe in an all-powerful God who is benevolent and can give purpose to our lives. People like the idea and so they make it true. If you were to take your preferred view of how a God might look, you'll find Christianity and other religions match your expectations of the ideal fairly well (Nicholi 2002). Freud seemed to rely on classical thinkers such as Sophocles,

Lucretius, and Socrates to describe the reasons he disbelieved in God. He also added his own twist to earlier theories by describing his Atheism in terms of psychoanalysis. Freud's view was that theism is an extension of relationships in our childhood - we just replace our parents with God. We remain children, helpless but protected and loved, forever.

Freud was influenced by the works of Ludwig Feuerbach, particularly the book "The Essence of Christianity" which was published in 1841. Feuerbach's work was adopted by a variety of famous and infamous thinkers such as Karl Marx.

In "The Essence of Christianity," he argues that all facets of God can be traced back to a human want or characteristic. He then takes this to the next step by saying if God has only human traits then God is indistinguishable from man and man becomes God (Feuerbach, L., & Eliot, G. 1893).

Feuerbach and Freud's views don't give enough credit to the roles of parents in indoctrination. Parents may intentionally attempt to indoctrinate their children, but they also influence the decisions of their children in a variety of other ways. It is relatively well-documented how parents guide their children towards or away from friendships and, ultimately, to a mate that meets their expectations. Parents demonstrate what it means to be a good partner, the values their children should look for in a potential mate, and often the religious views a mate should have. By acting as a model, parents are ensuring the continuation of their belief

Freud believed, at our core, we all hate our fathers (innately) and seek to overthrow them and take their power, what he called the Oedipus theory. Paul Vitz, in his book "Faith of the Fatherless," attempts to explain atheism using Freud's Oedipus theory: "Freud regularly described God as a psychological equivalent to the father, and so a natural expression of oedipal motivation would be powerful, unconscious desire for the nonexistence of God." Vitz seems to intend his explanation of atheism in these terms as a rebuke of Freud and his theories, but ultimately, I think he hits on something more fundamental. Most of the atheists I know seem to have a strong distrust for authority in any form. Fathers are the historical ultimate expression of authority. Accepting authority for the sake of authority is wrong-headed for many reasons, not the least of which is Hitler. It's important to note, though, my opinion is based on my experiences and not proper research. Also, as a side note on Paul Vitz's *Faith of the Fatherless*, I freely admit there is a lot wrong with his reasoning. He assumes positions without grounding and shows his biases early and often. Vitz writes in the same book, very near the quote above, "Those whose lives are characterized by promiscuity and atheism are, on Freud's analysis, living out the oedipal, primal rebellion."

The false association of atheists and promiscuity is cowardly… We get it, you're Catholic and atheists are an abomination. It is hard to take anyone seriously when they recite the same point over and over without supporting it with logic and reason. Still, his points about authority are supported. If Freud and Vitz are correct about the evolutionary roots of our movement away from father figures, it would make sense for those who discard authority to also discard God, as he is the ultimate expression of oppressive authority. It likely goes without saying, but I think having a distrust of authority is a wise state of being.

I have tried to instill in my children a healthy distrust in authority so they grow up questioning television ads and fight back against unethical demands. Teachers around the world claim authority on information they don't truly understand. In some cases, their students know more than they do (I can say this with confidence having taught college students for many years)! Parents are no different.

Uncovering knowledge from all around you is a wonderful way to learn. Businesses who allow information to flow across all levels are more likely to survive, and people who avoid accepting authority are less likely to be duped. So, thank you Paul Vitz, your observation was a wonderful source of knowledge, but I still don't accept your authority on the matter (Vitz 2013).

Parents, of course, are not operating in a vacuum - they had parents of their own and were raised in a community that encouraged the development of their beliefs. This community consists of friends, acquaintances, and businesses. Their social network may have been diverse, full of other ideas - or very limited. The influence of the social network and the context of the community on the transmission of belief cannot be understated.

A good example of this is the Duggars. They enforce a process of courtship wherein their daughters and sons are required to follow a ritualistic path to ensure that they find a mate who is of similar ideals and values. The parents have the ultimate authority to end any relationship or to reinforce any relationship they see as positive.

As I will discuss in the next section, a strongly reinforced social network of like-minded individuals, especially those attending the same church, guarantees continued indoctrination through the generations and encourages extremism as other idea systems are blocked out.

The Social Network

Everyone in the world belongs to a group of some kind or another. All of those groups have boundaries that determine who is in the group, and who is excluded from the group. Some people belong, some do not which is, in short, how groups work. In order to maintain group cohesion and encourage structure, the group has to have "group norms" and practices that reinforce those norms within the group. Groups perform a sort of regular and periodic self-regulation. Religious groups are very good at codifying their social norms and ensuring their group norms are met in a very systematic way. It is no surprise that religion is a part of so many social networks.

The research matches what common sense tells us. Religious groups self-police and are particularly effective at applying pressure on members to maintain the same beliefs and to maintain church attendance. In addition, if someone's friend group contains a high proportion of church-going friends, they are much more likely to attend - the more friends, the more pressure is placed on them to join their friends in attendance. As they attend, they become a part of the religious group, and they become more likely to take on the beliefs of that group. Being deeply embedded socially in a church also makes a person 27% more likely to become a biblical literalist and 23% more likely to believe theirs is the only "right" religion (Stroope 2016). As a person becomes engulfed in the social sphere of a religious community, their commitment, and actual belief increases. A study done in 2011 found belief can be influenced by the educational makeup of an individual church. It is relatively well known that individuals with more education are significantly less likely to be biblical literalists, but what this study found was, beyond the individual, when the church's educational makeup skews to less-educated, the entire congregation is significantly more likely to be biblically literal (Stroope 2011).

Journalist Jesse Singal once wrote, "...believing in seemingly strange things can be as simple as hanging out with other people who believe in those things." He was pointing to the power of social relationships in forming one's religious beliefs. Through interviews and research, he shows that when people are asked if they really believe all the tenets of their religion, people will generally say no and admit that in the quiet times away from social pressures, they chose only those parts of their religion they like. This pattern of picking and choosing is being emphasized in new forms of religion today (Singal, 2012).

However, conversion by peer pressure still happens. If a man were serving in the military and came home to find his friends all converted to a particular religion, he would be significantly more likely to convert. It is not the theology that is responsible for the conversion, but a want to be part of the group. The need to belong drives people into belief patterns. A 2005 study of Venezuelan men found "...life problems experienced by respondents were neither necessary nor sufficient causes of religious conversion (Smilde 2005)," but they also found that when men were having romantic trouble, or when they had asymmetry in their relationships, conversion was more likely. Couples with a social network dominated by a particular fundamental theology were likely to play along and a new biblical literalist may be born.

There are two ways the research above may be interpreted: The first is that like-minded individuals tend to stick together and therefore end up in the same church. In such a case, as these birds of a feather flock together, they encourage each other to continue to hold similar beliefs - or develop them in order to conform. The other, more sinister, way to look at it is that these groups and their individuals are in a "race to the bottom." By this view, the lowered education, and the likely biblical literalism, of the majority of the congregation can drag down those who are educated and damage their ability to think and behave rationally. The entire church races to a fundamentalist view and is less likely to subscribe to an evidenced-based world view.

In modern times, regular attendance of a church has become secondary to the more ethereal platform of social media. A younger generation of "spiritual" individuals are engaging their theology through the internet and their religious communities are founded in social media. Heidi Campbell from Texas A&M said, "We have more access to more information, more viewpoints, and we can create a spiritual rhythm and path that's more personalized (Stokel-Walker 2017)." They are looking for a God who makes sense to them and so they pick and choose the bits of religion they prefer. They leave on the shelf the things that do not jibe with their world view and take home those things that do. It's shopping cart religion - they are making their own faith.

Obviously, shopping cart religion does away with any literal interpretation of a holy book by necessity. Further, it does away with the notion of "truth" being contained in a single source. Instead, people are relying on their moral intuition to decide what they believe is right and wrong. With no truth and no holy book, there isn't much religion left. It is just people who don't believe in any current religion. In a way, the modern shopping cart religious are atheists who use religious materials as a way of describing what they already believe. They then share their revisionist beliefs through social media, which are read as alternatives to standard theology, and religion evolves. In the 1999 study on the transmission of parental belief, they stated that exposure to diverse beliefs was linked to lower dogmatism and a more personal belief system - and that is exactly what social media provides.

However, social media also gives arm-chair preachers and typically close-knit dogmatic communities a wider audience. Individuals who are not associated with structured religions, intentionally or unintentionally, gather followers who like their messages. The diverse experiences of these followers force the message of religion to change. The Church as a physical institution can no longer control the tenets of their faith completely. The authority of a single member of the clergy over their flock is waning. The social network of religion is evolving, and society is still struggling to adapt.

Society and Religion

Religion, like a contagious disease, can be spread around the world simply through contact between one society and the next. Catching the religious bug can occur through the transmission of ideas via "expansion" or through "relocation." Expansion happens when an idea spreads from person to person across geographical distances. Physical barriers, like distance or large bodies of water, can prevent the dispersion of religion. To overcome the obstacles many religions, use missionaries, sending people all over the world to spread the faith. They plant the seed in a new area and watch a new forest grow out of that single seed.

Missionaries also expand religion by relocating. A group who lived in an area with a particular religion moves to a new area and they bring their ideas with them. A fantastic example is the Mormons. When they went West, they brought

Mormonism with them. In the process, they displaced a variety of animistic religions that existed in the region at the time. The process of transmitting religions across society is relatively obvious. Imagine a missionary traveling to a new country and attempting to convert the leader of that country. If the missionary offers or seems to possess some sort of benefit such as education, monetary aid, or a promise of a better life and afterlife, the leader may be convinced to convert. From there, the leader's example - and policies - apply pressure across his entire nation to convert. The social network is changed from the top down.

There are two types of pressures that society puts on people, "direct" and "indirect." Indirect pressure occurs through the social hierarchy - people want to emulate other people who are in higher positions. Direct pressure uses legal or military force to push religious conversion. There have been many examples in the history of governments or peoples forcing citizens, often children, to subscribe to a specific set of beliefs. I will share some examples below as an illustration, but it's only the tip of the iceberg as it would take a whole set of books just to run through the examples.

The conversion of Emperor Constantine in ancient Rome is a perfect example of direct and indirect pressure in action. Constantine was the first Christian emperor in Rome. He built churches, lavished wealth on the Christian establishment, legitimized Christianity, and kicked off the Christianization of the Roman Empire. Christianity was later made the official religion of Rome. Constantine's conversion to Christianity seemed utilitarian at its outset, though it later became complete. He had claimed to see a sign of a Cross in the clouds that encouraged him to conquer in the name of Christianity. After a few successful battles, Constantine began to associate victory with the Christianity and began to make

Christian imagery (the Chi-Rho on the shields of his troops) and prayer a regular part of his battle strategy (MacCulloch, 2009).

In contrast, Judaism is notably not a religion of proselytization. The Jewish faith is generally passed down directly from parent (or extended family) to child, and conversion is usually difficult and not encouraged. Modern examples of Jews forcing others to join their religion are nearly nonexistent. However, there have been some incidences where Jews forcibly converted other religions. In the year 524, a Yemeni Christian tribe was given the option of conversion to Judaism or death. The incident resulted in what was approximated as 20,000 dead Christians. There may be other incidences, too, but for the most part, Jews end up with the short end of the stick as forced conversions go - Indeed, Yemeni Jews were later the subject of forced conversions in 1919, after Turkish rule of Yemen ended. The new ruling class in Yemen decided to enforce something known as the "orphans' decree". The orphans' decree required Jewish children, whose parents were dead and who were still underage, to be forcibly converted to Islam. Conversion occurred regardless of whether the orphans had family available to care for them after their parents died. The Jewish community in Yemen attempted to prevent forced conversion by hiding the children, treating them much like paupers in a sort of social welfare network. Other strategies to avoid this law included marrying-off the children at a young age, passing the orphans off as children from a different family, or smuggling them out of the country. The practice of forced conversion continued, officially, until the 1940s, but may have continued unofficially much longer (Gaimani 2004).

In 14th and 15th century Spain, Jewish citizens were forced to convert to Catholicism by the rulers of the time,

Ferdinand and Isabella. The orders were to convert to Catholicism or leave the country entirely. Many Jews, known as conversos, chose to convert to Catholicism in order to maintain their position within society. Ultimately, however, the Spanish ruling class found their conversions to be untrustworthy and not of pure intentions. They felt as though the conversos were undermining Catholicism from within. This mistrust, born of their own policies, eventually led to the horrors of the Spanish Inquisition. By integrating the conversos into the Catholic Church the Spaniards managed to create a problem that they then sought to solve through the harshest of means.

People have even been forcibly converted into atheism, despite this being against the very fundamentals of atheism! In the former Soviet Union and in modern communist countries like China the lack of religion is considered the official religion and religious affiliations are frowned upon. While China uses social pressure to indirectly encourage the "practice" of atheism, the former Soviet Union, by contrast, actually took direct and brutal action against religious adherents. They persecuted believers with police and military. The Russian Orthodox Church, in particular, was made into a target. According to the Revelations from the Russian Archives as presented by the Library of Congress, "Nearly all of its [The Russian Orthodox Church] clergy, and many of its believers, were shot or sent to labor camps ("Anti-religious Campaigns," n.d.-a)." In a letter from Maxim Gorky to Stalin, Gorky wrote:

> "It is furthermore imperative to put the propaganda of atheism on solid ground. You won't achieve much with the weapons of Marx and materialism, as we have seen. Materialism and religion are two different planes and they don't coincide. If a

fool speaks from the heavens and the sage from a factory--they won't understand one another. The sage needs to hit the fool with his stick, with his weapon.

For this reason, there should be courses set up at the Communist Academy which would not only treat the history of religion, and mainly the history of the Christian church, i.e., the study of church history as politics.

We need to know the "fathers of the church," the apologists of Christianity, especially indispensable to the study of the history of Catholicism, the most powerful and intellectual church organization whose political significance is quite clear. We need to know the history of church schisms, heresies, the Inquisition, the "religious" wars, etc. Every quotation by a believer is easily countered with dozens of theological quotations which contradict it.

We cannot do without an edition of the "Bible" with critical commentaries from the Tubingen school and books on criticism of biblical texts, which could bring a very useful "confusion into the minds" of believers ("Anti-religious Campaigns," n.d.-b)."

Christians forcibly converted Jews, Jews converted Christians and Muslims, Muslims converted Jews and Christians, and atheists have converted all faiths. Really, no group is without blame on some level. I obviously do not agree with the communist brand of forced atheism: I believe atheism is right on its own accord and should be deeply considered and subject to questioning. People should be allowed to learn any and all religious traditions and choose their own path. I don't think children should have religion forced upon them, just as I don't believe they should have atheism forced upon them. All humans deserve the right to choose their own path of belief, free of direct governmental intervention. May the best ideas win.

The indirect influence of societal pressure leads to indoctrination and is more subtle than labor camps, but just as effective in many ways. For example, where we are born matters greatly. Being born in a Christian nation means you are more likely to be born Christian, though the severity of Christianity matters. Europe is becoming increasingly progressive and the societal pressure to remain Christian is lessening. Europe is liberalizing and the young are balking at traditional religion. According to a study recently reported in the Guardian, "Only in Poland, Portugal and Ireland did more than 10% of young people say they attend services at least once a week (Sherwood, 2018)." More and more, Western society is encouraging people to look inwards for their faith.

Aspirational Beliefs and Self Discovery

When membership in a specific group seems to be a path to prosperity or social standing, people are more likely to want to join. Freemasonry and their networking are a good example. Freemasons started as a group of craftsmen who wished to improve and grow their craft. They instituted apprenticeships and recruited talent. Those who joined often saw an economic benefit and the Masons continued to grow through the centuries, developing rites and symbols along the way. The Freemasons still exist today and membership in their group has many social benefits. They assist each other in life and prosperity (Zimmer 2017).

Churches are not terribly different from the Freemasons, as much as the Catholic Church would hate to admit it. They both have formal ceremonies, provide networks for their members, and have places of observance. Those who wish to be prosperous in society may feel the need to join a church in order to advance their wellbeing and it seems as though people are aware of this fact. Those who are religious and prosperous share their success and beliefs more broadly than those who are not prosperous. The wealthier the believer, the louder the believer (Cornwall 1998).

Societies, friends, and parents are all influencers of our religious beliefs, but many people also find their beliefs by turning inward. People may choose a belief based on their aspirations, like joining the Masons, or through a journey of self-discovery that leads them to a view they believe to be right. First, it is important to note that conversion is not the primary way people find religion. Conversions are relatively rare, making up perhaps 0.7% of religious people on the high side. According to a study on the rates of religious conversions by Barro and Hwang conversions are much lower where religions are more "state-orientated (Barro & Hwang, 2007)." Still, they are the only way to understand why people choose their religion. If a person didn't convert, then they must have been part of the indoctrination machine described above. Conversion experiences are often assessed through surveys. Surveying is not without its flaws. People responding to surveys do so in ways that are not always intellectually honest. After all, if you only went to see concerts from Depeche Mode because you had a girlfriend who was into them and you were surveyed at the time, there is a decent chance you wouldn't own up to just being at the concert for a girl. You might, on the other hand, say you found the music moving and that it filled a hole in your soul you didn't know you had until you learned about them. Twenty years later, you would likely come to your senses and have a very different reason. Is it possible people want to believe they converted to religion for better, more intellectual reasons then they actually did? Indeed, they may make their decisions irrationally and then later rationalize their reasons making survey studies notoriously inaccurate.

Still, through these studies, patterns emerge: often the most commonly cited reason (in the 60% range) for conversion was "seeking." People were looking to add meaning to their lives that they weren't finding on their own. These individuals often say they don't feel any social pressure to convert - the pressure comes from within. Their stories sound something like, "I didn't feel fulfilled in my life and wanted to find meaning" or "I was really depressed and needed to find a way out" or "I did a bunch of research and found my new religion." These conversions are more cerebral in nature. They represent self-discovery. For an atheist, the conversion experience is the same: "I was a churchgoer and felt unsatisfied. I started doubting God and ultimately realized there is no God." Discontent leads to deep thought which leads to self-discovery and a change in beliefs. I have a lot of respect for religious choice made through deep contemplation and self-discovery (Snook, Kleinmann, White, & Horgan, 2019).

Conversion studies also highlight the aspirational reasons people change religions, though they may not always characterize them as such. An early theory for why people convert was "relative deprivation theory" - individuals who feel deprived of money or social standing would seek improvement in their standing by finding a new religion where the adherents appear to be more successful. They see changing religion as a necessary step towards a better life

(Snook & Horgan 2019). Scientology is notorious for using aspirations, rather than faith, as leverage. They intentionally target celebrities for conversion as a sort of "conversion bait." Regular people see the celebrities and their success and think, "Scientology must be worth doing if it is helping such successful people!" The "church" of Scientology is hoping people aspire to be like celebrities and convert to their "religion -" which is primarily a for-profit enterprise (Grim, 2017).

At the end of all this discussion about how religion is passed through society, I want to return to atheism. Freud and many others have tried to explain atheism in their framework of understanding. The theories earlier in this chapter help to explain theism and its prevalence in society, but do we actually need a theory for atheism? I have trouble rationalizing a need for it. My position is that there is no need to explain atheism, just as there is no need to explain why people don't believe in the Easter Bunny or Santa. To say a theory is needed is to say the natural state of man is belief in a specific religion. For Christians, it's the assumption that everyone is built to believe in Christ. For some Muslims, the assumption is Islam. These assumptions are no truer than to say everyone is built to believe in the Easter Bunny.

As we have seen, time and time again, disbelief is the natural state of man and external forces move people away from their natural state… and then continue to evolve from there, as all memes do.

Chapter Seven: Religious Erosion

> "Religion of our conception, thus imperfect,
> is always subject to a process of evolution
> and re-interpretation."
>
> *Mahatma Gandhi*

> "There is only one religion, though there are
> a hundred versions of it."
>
> *George Bernard Shaw*

The term "religious erosion" is used a lot in popular culture, and it evokes feelings of governmental overreach and the encroachment of civil liberties, as in the erosion of religious freedom or religious liberty. People use the concept of religious erosion to rile up groups of followers around the idea that their freedoms are in jeopardy. Here, I will use the term religious erosion to mean the process by which the tenets of a religion change, and liberalize over time - how it evolves. I don't mind using the same, smart term to invoke feelings of the loss of religious convictions. The difference is that I see it as a natural process. A process where the changes in a religion have been "naturally selected." All religions with any significant following have had to adapt, change...*erode* in some way to keep up with a changing world.

For example, where there was a precept around no women in church facilities, now there are women ministers. The idea of women as an "other" has gradually eroded in the Church. The erosion, this change in practice, is very good for both the Church and society as a whole. We are all watching as the Church evolves to meet the expectations of the people it serves, just like any business would. Because of these changes, the Church today is not a Church the apostles of Christ would recognize. It is something new and different. As an atheist, the erosion of religious precepts confirms my understanding of religion as a social construct rather than a revealed truth. I don't need to worry that I will be cut by Occam's razor and be on the wrong side of Pascal's wager. It is one more way I can be confident that I have chosen the right path. I hope one day, the whole thing will erode away much like a mountain can be eroded into a plain. I just hope it doesn't take as long. This chapter will explore the ways in which religion has eroded over the years.

Erosion occurs in four main forms, though all are erosions of authority in one sense or another: the erosion of the church, of practice, of ignorance, or of the revealed texts. In each case the fundamental tenets of the religion change. In the example of erosion of the church, you might find the Church's authority being changed as a result of modern sensibilities. In the example of erosion of the revealed texts, you might find portions of the Bible being discarded as modern science erodes its infallibility. I will delve into each of the areas in turn.

Erosion of the Church

Churches, as institutions from all religions, have been eroding for a long time. They have eroded in obvious ways and less obvious ways. The erosion has occurred through the loss of power across religious institutions. Historically, Churches have acted as political and spiritual institutions. When they have lost power, it has been through losing followers, influence, the moral high-ground, and the hearts and minds of churchgoers. A more recent development is the degradation of Church attendance, the cornerstone of the religious indoctrination process.

The erosion of church attendance is a relatively new phenomenon. In the 1700s, attendance at churches was estimated to be between 70% to 80% in America (Religion and the founding of the American republic., Library of Congress). That level of attendance continued until the 1980s. In the late 80s the rate of church membership began to decline and has continued to decline ever since. The rate dropped into the high 60 percents in the 90s. After the turn of the millennium, the rate started to drop more quickly, 64% in 2003, 61% in 2008 (Pew Research Center, 2014) and all the way down to 55% by 2013. In 2018, the rate was down to 50% in the United States according to a Gallup poll (Jones, 2019).

Younger generations appear to be moving away from religion as a whole. The percentage of Americans who identified as having no religion around 2000 was only 8%, by 2018 this number climbed to 19%. The decline in church membership between 2000 and 2018 varied by generation, although all generations saw declines. The younger the cohort the less likely they were to be church members. For example, 68% of those born in 1945 or earlier were still Church members in 2018, while the church membership of those born from 1980 to 2000 was as low as 42%. There is a corresponding generational difference between Millennials and those born in 1945 or earlier when it comes to religiosity as a whole. Only 9% of those born in 1945 or earlier identified as non-religious in 2018, while 29% of Millennials identified as non-religious. The Gallup researchers felt there was a correlation between the declines in religiosity and church membership. An earlier study noted Americans continue to hit all-time lows in their confidence in organized religion

(Jones, 2019). Only 38% of respondents to their survey felt a great deal of confidence in churches. For years the survey identified churches as the most trusted institutions in America. They have fallen precipitously (Saad, 2018).

People's confidence in the church has been shaken as society recognizes that church teachings lag behind the evolving morality of modernity. Some examples are too easy to name and don't bear a detailed retelling here. The abuse of children in the Catholic Church, the many sex scandals of modern megachurches, the treatment of women and the LGBTQ community are all potential causes of the decreasing confidence and attendance in churches.

There was also a major flight away from the Catholic church as a result of the papal encyclical - a letter sent to all bishops of the church - that upheld the long-standing tradition of prohibiting birth control back in the late 1960s. Many of the Catholic religious adherents who felt the Church was off base went to other, more accepting religions. The timing was portentous as the encyclical was released around the same time as the Second Vatican Council (known as Vatican II).

Vatican II was diverse and had attendants from many different churches and it began a process of liberalization in the Catholic Church. The Church began to modernize, including a move towards performing Mass in the native language of the congregation and acceptance of other Catholic institutions. Through these measures, the Pope attempted to make the Catholic Church more accessible to the average person around the world. Meanwhile, however, they continued to oppose birth control, hindering their efforts. These anachronistic views led to a flight away from Catholicism in the late sixties and early seventies.

Continually changing the precepts of religion is one of many ways in which modern humans flex their religious choice and, conversely, how churches change in order to be chosen. To use the terms of science, churches evolve to fit the needs of their parishioners. No church is static and that means no religion is static and, as such, no religion is the same as it was at the time of its founding. Religions are purely social constructs. There is nothing permanent or eternal about them (McCleary 2011).

From the beginning of Christianity, the Church has been eroding. If the original teachings of Christ can be said to be the origin of the first Church, then the changes to that church began almost immediately after his death. The Bible itself is a mish-mosh of accounts that differ in small and large ways. It is important to remember the Bible was compiled at least half a century after the death of Christ. Before then, traditions were passed on orally, which of course leads to the message changing like a game of telephone.

Christian factions were forming almost from year one of the common era. The beliefs of these Christian factions differed on things like the nature of Jesus Christ, his teachings, and the right way to worship and live. The factions changed the Church. Rather than the slow change of church policy described above, the changes were massive as the church branched to create new sects. The diversity of stories and writings were notable and Christendom tried to reign in their difference by coming together in large cross-denominational meetings called ecumenical councils. The first of these councils occurred in the year 325C.E. at what came to be known as the Council of Nicea (MacCulloch, 2009).

Prior to the council, there was a debate raging in the Christian community about the nature of Jesus. Was he a God, part of *the* God, created by God for a purpose, a mortal prophet, or just a man? Constantine, in an effort to galvanize Christianity for political gain, wanted to end the debate and convened a council of Christian leaders to debate what came to be known as the Arian controversy, named after Arius, a priest from Alexandria. Arius wrote that the Son was not part of the Father as he was born and had a definite beginning. The prevailing wisdom was that Jesus was part of God, not a separate entity. The Arian view was voted down by the council and Arius was exiled as were other dissenters, but the split in interpretation persisted and new areas of disagreement arose.

Many more councils were held throughout the years and in each instance the church tried to solidify its power and prevent further fractionation. Ultimately, however, even this coordinated effort was unable to stop the spread of new interpretations. Some notable splits within the church occurred around the following items:

- The nature of Mary, Jesus' mother - First Council of Ephesus (431 A.D.)

- Whether images of Jesus or God could be used in churches - They were okay in the Second Council of Nicaea (787 A.D.), and they were outlawed in the Fourth Council of Constantinople (869-870 A.D.)

- The role of the state within the Church - First Council of the Lateran (1123 A.D.)

- Celibacy of clergy - First Council of the Lateran (1123 A.D.)

- Usury (the practice of charging interest) - Third Council of the Lateran (1179)

- Transubstantiation (wherein the bread and wine of communion turns into the literal body and blood of christ) - Fourth Council of the Lateran (1215)

There were a variety of other changes that occurred through the councils. Many of them led to split-off sects of Christianity as ideas were either rejected or accepted as part of the ecumenical process. Politics and theology drove the need for additional sectarianism, as was the case with the Great Schism (also known as the East-West schism) where the church split between Eastern Orthodoxy and Catholicism. The split was driven largely by a struggle for authority between Rome and Constantinople, but there were undertones of Arianism as the Church fought over the relationship between God the Father and Jesus as his son.

The combination of the political divide and theological disagreement caused a split in the church that still exists, creating the two largest individual Church entities. Throughout the various ecumenical councils, as the formal church authorities tried to reign in interpretations, more and more sects and orders were created. The reformation kicked off an even faster pace of sectarianism as protestants began their moves away from the Catholic and Orthodox churches.

The trend of splitting continues today - some estimate the number of Christian denominations as high as 47,000 and growing. According to a survey of Christianity conducted by the Gordon Cromwell Theological Seminary, the number of Christian denominations grew from 1600 in 1900 to over 18,000 by 1970 and up to 45,000 in 2019. The number is expected to continue to grow up to 64,000 by 2050 (Bashir,

Nelson, & Burbank, 2009). Even with a conservative number of 10,000 denominations, the variation from group to group in practice and belief can be huge. While the central figure in Christian sects is Jesus, much else can differ.

Think about the differences between Mormons and Catholics or Unitarians and Mennonites. There are those who believe in Christ as a human prophet and those who see him as God. Some sects believe in the clergy as a conduit to God, some believe God is personal and can't be found in organized churches. This variation allows the religious to pick and choose any mixture they like and if they don't like their options, there seem to be very few barriers to creating your own sect. God is made by people, not the other way around.

Erosion of the Practice

Religion today is, in many ways, very different from what it was for much of history. We see religion as an entity that is separate from many aspects of life where it wasn't in earlier times. For example, there are periods in history where the Church was nearly solely responsible for the education of the population. Universities and primary education were often sponsored and conducted by the church and its clergy. This is still true in parts of the world today. Even in the United States, there are many religious educational institutions. According to the National Center for Education Statistics, 67% of private schools have a religious affiliation. The enrollment in religious schools makes up about 7% of all enrollment in elementary and secondary schools in the United States (Broughman, Rettig, & Peterson, 2017; National Center for Education Statistics, N.D.).

Just as with education, the role of religious institutions in medicine, and social welfare has changed dramatically. In ancient times, religious institutions were the main source of medical healing. For example, the Greco-Roman temples of the Gods also functioned as medical and healing centers. The tradition continued for centuries.

Christian churches, in particular, Catholic churches were bastions of medical healing into the Middle Ages. The same is true of Islamic temples, where some great strides in medical technology were made. The secularization of religious medical facilities didn't occur until the late 18th and into the 19th centuries when there was an increase in state-run or privately owned medical facilities (Porter, 2017). Today we recognize it is no longer necessary to have religion as part of Medicine, but rather we benefit far more when the two entities remain entirely separate.

When the two are joined it can cause problems because religion muddies the process of medical healing. For example, Christian Scientists try to avoid medicine because they believe it goes against God's will even if it means sick or dying children, which makes sense if you assume that God has a plan for each individual and human intervention can only get in the way of those plans (Dentzer, 2016; Paul Vitello, 2010). Patients' religion may inform their care choices, but don't impact clinical recommendations for treatment. There is a point where a patient needs to be protected from themselves or a parent. We recognize the need to intervene in cases of mental illness. Is there an allegory for the religious? A 2009 article in the American Medical Association Journal of Ethics recounts just how hard it is to find the right point of intervention. "Iraqi physician Nabil Al-Khalisi recounts a clinical tragedy in which a child with methanol poisoning dies because the physician cannot convince the child's grandfather that ingesting alcohol ethanol [used to counteract methenol], prohibited by the grandfather's understanding of Islamic law, is an effective therapy (Shinall, 2009)."

Where is the line drawn when it comes to intervening to save a human life? Perhaps it's assisting in a suicide, a mortal sin in Christianity, or maybe it's enough to avoid treating a sick or dying person, even if it is at their request. Is it going against God's will to treat the person in the first place, preventing His ultimate plan of letting the person die from disease? With all of these complicated questions being raised, it makes sense that the church has eroded away its ability to offer reasonable Medical Care as science has usurped its authority and knowledge. I don't mean to diminish the value of what the Church has done for modern medicine, but rather to note that modern medicine has discarded the need for Church, just as the Church has lost its authority within medicine.

Other church practices, such as confession and communion, have changed quite a bit or were removed completely in the case of Protestantism. For many hundreds of years, both were tenets of the Church that were unquestioned. Confession and communion seemed to be a necessity of faith. Confession, in particular, was not under the aegis of the Church during the beginning of Christianity. There are several Biblical passages that suggest confession is a necessary part of being a Christian, but most of the passages refer to confessing your sins either to your neighbors or to God directly. For example, James 5:16 says, "Confess your faults one to another, and pray one for another, that ye may be healed," and there is a passage in Psalm 32:5 that says, "I said, I will confess my transgressions unto the Lord; and thou forgavest the iniquity of my sin (King James Version)." Confessing to a priest came much later. Priestly confession was something the church created in order to maintain control over the religious life of their parishioners.

Just like a business trying to maintain their customer base, they had to ensure customers kept going back. Communion and confession were two reasons a church-goer would have to visit the church frequently, where they could be involved in other facets of the church. The Catholic Church made confession one of their Sacraments in their catechisms - a summary of the principles of the Catholic faith - circa 1456: "Confession to a priest is an essential part of the sacrament of penance." With confession codified, Catholic priests became the arbiters of parishioners' entrance into heaven, giving priests control over their eternal lives. Owning access to heaven cemented the church's power and ensured a constant stream of revenue as church-goers came in for confession and, likely more importantly, tithing.

As corruption undermined the trustworthiness of priests as gatekeepers of heaven, Protestantism rose up, doing away with what seemed like key practices of Christianity at the time, like communion, the station of the Pope, and a variety of other Catholic mainstays. Religious people lost faith in the priests' abilities to act as a vessel of God when the priests themselves were so clearly taking advantage of their positions. Protestantism reflects yet another way in which the church has changed to meet the needs of the people they serve.

Marriage is just another way that the church has shown that it is really a social force, not a puritanistic system of beliefs that are immutable. We commonly associate marriage and religion today, but that was not always the case. Marriage and weddings predated modern Abrahamic religion. They have been around for recorded history in many different forms. Arranged marriages were common for political reasons or dowry (Coontz, 2005). In fact, marriage was such a mainstay in society that the contemporaries of Jesus didn't make it important in their teachings. The only passage in the old testament that speaks to a husband and wife referred to their union as one person: "Therefore a man leaves his father and his mother and clings to his wife, and they become one flesh (Genesis 2:24)." In the new testament there are references to Jesus attending weddings, but not much else.

The Church adopted marriage and added additional rules and rites in an effort to control the lives of the parishioners. It wasn't even until 1215 that the church added marriage as one of the sacraments, but even after the acceptance into the sacraments the church continued to accept the word of the married couple that they were in fact wed, no other evidence or service was needed. Marriage didn't become officially part of the church until it became a requirement for priests to participate, only about 500 years ago in the 1500s (Harmon 2018).

Polygamy (the practice or custom of having more than one wife or husband at the same time) is an excellent case study on how religious practices have morphed to fit the sensibilities of the times. Many of the figures in the Bible were polygamous such as David, Solomon, and Jacob. Kings and noblemen practiced polygamy for thousands of years. It was only in the 9th century that the Catholic church pushed it to the fringe and discontinued the practice for adherents (Ghose, 2013). Still, polygamy exists around the world today, even in Christian-dominant countries, though it is frowned upon in Western culture. Polygamy is particularly interesting because the earliest sects of Christianity and Judaism actually condoned polygamy. It wasn't until society moved away from the idea of polygamy that the Church's stance changed and monogamy became the norm.

Over the years, the waffling back and forth on the religious nature of marriage has caused the church to overstep in many ways. Today, the Church's authority around marriage is continuously changing, especially when it comes to gay marriage and marriage outside the confines of the church. People are getting married in churches less and less, and marriage-free lifestyles and secular marriage have gained popularity. A religious website called the Religion News Service said it this way, "Religion is the great loser in that revolution, not only ceding its cultural influence but also struggling to govern the lifestyle choices of its own adherents (Status of global christianity, 2019, in the context of 1900–2050.2019)."

Marriage, as a social institution, is on the decline. Less people are marrying and more are cohabiting (Lupfer, 2018). According to U.S. census bureau data, the percent of Americans who cohabitate and are unmarried increased by nearly 30% from 2007 to 2016 with the biggest increase coming from Americans 50 years or older (Stepler 2017). The church's authority for marriage will probably continue to erode as time passes and global society becomes more progressive overall - a trajectory that doesn't seem to be slowing.

Erosion of Mystery

Religion relies on the mystery of the Universe, and that mystery begins to erode as we understand more and more of it. The Church has been forced to defend itself against being altered as a result of scientific advancement time and time again. The erosion of religion after the improved understanding of the Universe and the world around us is a softball for an atheist - There are too many examples to discuss them all. To keep the process simple, I will again only cite three different examples. The first example of science eroding faith is likely one of the most well-known examples; the Copernican shift to a heliocentric view of the Universe. Heliocentrism is the idea that the Earth revolves around the sun, as opposed to the Earth being at the center of everything. The Geocentric, or Earth-centered, model supports a religious view of Earth, the planet of Humanity, being the center of a divine and perfect universe. The Heliocentric theory upsets this, proposing a non-Earthly, imperfect universe far less friendly to the divine. Two of the world's most famous scientists; Nicolaus Copernicus and Galileo Galilei, brought forth the heliocentric view and suffered for it.

Nicolaus Copernicus originally floated the idea based on his mathematical models which showed the Earth revolved around the sun and not the other way around. His idea was confirmed by Galileo Galilei with his observations of the motions of the stars and planets. In 1616, the church moved against Galileo and formed an Inquisition that determined the heliocentric view of the Universe was heretical. Pope Paul V ordered Galileo not to teach or defend his ideas and to abandon any further promotion of heliocentrism. The church's actions were based on the language of the Bible, a perfect example of religious officials adhering to a fallible book rather than observable scientific evidence. Later, Pope Urban VIII softened the church's stance. He tried to convince Galileo to present Heliocentrism and Geocentrism equally, without upsetting the balance of the Church. Galileo refused, defending the idea of heliocentrism as more reflective of the Universe.

Some viewed Galileo's response as demeaning to the Pope, which upset Pope Urban and eventually led to another trial. Galileo was placed under house arrest for the remainder of his life and forced to recant. Ironically, the heliocentric model was a significantly better predictor of calendar dates and times, and eventually would have to be adopted by the Church.

It's funny to think about the heliocentric example in the context of today, where no reasonable person would believe that the Earth is at the center of either the Universe or the solar system. Geocentrism is so obviously false, holding an opposing viewpoint would sound absurd. Though the Bible does speak to the prominence of Earth within the Universe, especially in Genesis, even today's church recognizes that the Earth is not at the center of the Galaxy and the biblical references are seen as metaphorical rather than literal. Those who say otherwise are written off as raving and fearful religious traditionalists.

A second example of the church's degradation due to scientific advancement is our improved understanding of the age of the Earth. The Bible seems to suggest a definite age for the Earth, something close to 6,000 years, but science has clearly shown the Earth to be significantly older - on the order of *Billions* of years. Much like the heliocentric view of the world, this was a change in the way society saw our Earth, in the context of the larger Universe. It directly challenged the literal interpretation of the Bible. Today, the Catholic church has been forced to accept a metaphorical interpretation of any passages that might refer to the age of the Earth. The most common and accurate method for calculating the age of the Earth is currently radiometric dating where the radioactive decay of elements is used as a sort of clock. The radioactive clock ticks at a constant rate and can be traced back to when it began, around 4.5 billion years ago (Bryner, 2012). Instead, as stated by the Pope, the Church "lets" individuals decide on their own what to believe about the age of the Earth. They hold strong with the idea that both the Earth and the Universe are finite because God created them, but the church has adapted to the changing times: it doesn't feel the age of the Earth has to follow a chronological reading of the Bible. Pope Pius VII cautioned against literal readings of the Bible, saying that in ancient times the metaphor was more important than the exact facts and timelines. The ancients, he claimed, were likely not trying to give a direct answer to the age of the Earth. He also said ancient people may not have had the right words to describe the passage of time, especially when it comes to billions of years. He said:

"For the ancient peoples of the east, in order to express their ideas, did not always employ those forms or kinds of speech which we use today; but rather those used by men of their times in their countries (Catholic Answers 2019)."

The 6,000-year-old Earth is also a fairly recent concept. It was proposed in the 17th century by a few different sources but most notably an Archbishop, James Ussher, who followed biblical timelines to determine the age (Bressan, 2013; MacCulloch, 2009). He had to do some mental and mathematical gymnastics in order to arrive at a date, relying on a variety of sources. There is no place in the Bible where it directly gives the age of the Earth or the larger Universe. Ussher relied on evidence from the other limited ancient texts available for his scholarly review. Ussher's goal was to use available textual information to work out an age for the Earth and join ideas from the various sources to create a timeline of events. His work doesn't seem to be inherently theistic, though it lent credence to religious arguments and was used for centuries. In all, only about a sixth of his calculations used the Bible directly (Smith, N.D.). After Ussher's calculation, the debate about the age of the Earth continued for centuries among religious officials.

The debate hasn't fully ended: Today we actually have a split between what is often referred to as "Young-Earth Creationism" and "Old-Earth Creationism." The Young-Earthers cling to the idea that the Earth is only 6,000 years old while the Old-Earthers accept the science as fact, the Earth is billions of years old, but with the caveat of a "Prime Mover." The concept of a "Prime Mover" is that there was a spark, or Big Bang, triggered by God that set the whole Universe in motion. The Old-Earthers consider the Bible to be a metaphorical truth, not meant to be read literally, and the rift between them and the Young Earthers - who are Bible literalists - continues to grow. Some Young-Earthers claim Old-Earthers are not truly Christian because of their differences, yet another example of disunity and dysfunction within the faith (O'Neil 2014).

The Catholic Church is very progressive to allow such flexibility. Christian, and even some Jewish and Islamic, fundamentalists do not permit a metaphorical reading of their holy books. The conflict arising from the differences between religious and scientific views of the formation of our Earth has become an important part of our society. Underlying the conflict is a strong need to understand our planet. Our scientific understanding of the world has led us to make conclusions about how the Earth was formed and, just as importantly, how it may behave in the future. It has helped us understand where to look for oil or how the plates of the Earth move and impact all of us "surface-dwellers" with Earthquakes, volcanic eruptions, and other titanic events.

Understanding the age of the Earth has also helped us

recognize our significance, (or insignificance) within the Universe which is very important as we try to navigate off-planet with new technologies and advancements in science. In time, a billions-of-years-old Earth will likely be just as accepted as the heliocentric view of the solar system. The continued support of a more metaphorical interpretation of the Bible will continue to erode the church and its authority and trustworthiness within society. People want the benefits of science, benefits that religion is no longer able to provide. I believe society's want for the benefits of science will ultimately lead to continued flight away from the Church.

Having started with a universe sized problem and moved to a planet-sized problem, I want to next explore an even smaller scale issue, a human-sized problem. Lord Kelvin was a creationist who, having read Darwin's *Origin of Species*, felt strongly the Earth was not old enough to allow for the evolution Charles Darwin believed caused the large diversity that exists on Earth today. In his estimate, the age of the Earth was between 20 and 40 million years, which was significantly longer than the 6,000-year literalist age of the Earth. Ironically his attempts at refuting Darwinism ultimately led to advancements that further undermined his argument.

The debate over evolution itself can be used as an example. It is still an ongoing discussion in American culture, though it really shouldn't be. Movies have been made, books have been written, debates have raged, and the theory of evolution has been repeatedly proven as a scientific law of the Universe... And yet we still talk about it! The religious fervor against the idea of evolution drives the conversation.

The Catholic Church's position on evolution is actually a somewhat middle-ground position. They seem to allow for the idea of evolution in some cases and even accept it in others, but they still reinforce the infallibility of biblical texts.

The Bible is relatively silent on creation, unless you consider the biblical timelines within Genesis to be literally true. If you do, then Man was created in a single day, not over the millions of years necessary for evolution. If instead, you read Genesis as a metaphor, evolution as a scientific fact can persist. As a consequence, even observant Catholics often believe in God-guided-evolution. According to a 2014 Pew Research Center report, up to 68% of Catholics (depending on race) believe in evolution and half of those who believe in evolution believe it was guided by God (*Public's views on human evolution;2014 SRI R8584-46.*2014).

The biblical literalist world view is a problem not just because the evidence for evolution is clear and irrefutable but because evolution makes predictions that are exceedingly useful in our daily lives. Understanding the workings of evolution and natural selection in detail has allowed us to make incredible advancements in science and medicine which have improved the lives of millions of people around the world. Everyone enjoys the improvements regardless of their religious beliefs. Religious and irreligious alike have better health due to research into the evolution of infectious and genetic diseases and the evolution of the human immune system. Millions, perhaps billions, around the world have been pulled out of hunger by the study of plant genetics (from breeding to direct genetic modification).

Yet, the argument continues. We fight over whether evolution is a "theory" or a fact, whether the evidence that supports it is real, and what place evolution has in the curriculum at our schools. In some states we even argue about whether evolution should be taught at all. We argue so much that we have to take the argument to the highest of courts! When judges are forced to weigh in on the evidence, they always side with the fact that evolution is clearly supported by the evidence and should be taught to our children. Religious adherents try to dance around the idea by employing unsupportable concepts, like "Intelligent Design," that rely on the gaps in people's understanding. These so-called "Christian Scientists" use an approach which exploits ignorance, reinforces group identity and plays on people's emotions. They say, "Have you ever seen evolution happen? Have you seen a monkey turn into a person? Good Christians can't believe in evolution, and besides, your uncle wasn't a monkey, was he?"

In an article posted on the website for The Institute for Creation Research, there are few quotes which illustrate the examples above:

- "...the billions of known fossils do not include a single unequivocal transitional form with transitional structures in the process of evolving."

- "...the lack of a case for evolution is clear from the fact that no one has ever seen it happen. If it were a real process, evolution should still be occurring, and there should be many "transitional" forms that we could observe."

- "The entire history of evolution from the evolution of life from non-life to the evolution of vertebrates from invertebrates to the evolution of man from the ape is strikingly devoid of intermediates: the links are all missing in the fossil record, just as they are in the present world."

These passages were written by Henry M. Morris, Ph.D. who was a hydraulics engineer by education and trade.

Morris is sometimes considered the father of Young-Earth creationism (Morris, n.d.).

These apparent gaps in knowledge are easily bridged by science. There are transitional fossils, and irreducible complexity doesn't exist. The gaps are just gaps in the understanding of individuals. The literalists are preying on the less informed rather than trying to share all the facts. Dogmatic interpretations allow them to ignore any evidence that is contradictory to their beliefs and perpetuates the idea that evolution may not actually be settled. All of the conjecture is irrelevant considering we have actually observed evolution take place!

We have seen small scale examples of evolution based on human activity such as an increase in the percentage of newborn elephants without tusks because we humans love ivory or birds with shorter wings to avoid getting hit by our cars (Fred W. Allendorf & Jeffrey J. Hard, 2009). We have also seen major changes in animals. One of the most troubling recent evolutionary trends is the rise of drug resistant bacteria which arises from the quick evolution of bacteria that become able to survive antibiotics. The Washington post produces a running column called "Dear Science." In one response to readers' questions about evolution, they shared the following example of an observed change to a transitional species complete with a little punctuated equilibrium:

> "About a century ago, a few British mosquitoes found themselves lost in the tunnels of the London Underground. Trapped beneath the Earth, they foraged for food, searched for mates, and became so well-adapted to their subterranean habitat that they became genetically distinct. They eat different prey and

>require different climate conditions than other mosquitoes. When scientists tried to cross breed them with their above-ground counterparts, the eggs were infertile — evidence that a new species, Culex molestus, had emerged. Evolution in action, right beneath our feet (Feltman & Kaplan, 2016)."

It is easy to see how evolution has eroded the authority of the church. If the religious creationists would embrace evolution instead of fighting against it, they would likely be able to hold on to their position within society - which is what the Catholic church has done. Instead, churches fight against what causes change, because any change in the Church contradicts the idea of an unchanging, static universe created by God and given to humans to do with as they please.

We have moved past the idea that the Bible can give us any useful information to aid in scientific advancement or discovery. After all, the Bible is really just a transcribed oral history. Science and religion cannot be separated as long as religion claims authority over scientific ideas. They cannot be non-overlapping magisteria - completely separate and operating in different spheres of influence - as proposed by Stephen Jay Gould. The idea that science should be concerned with "how" and faith should answer "why" might make sense, if only the religious stopped trying to take over the how, too... though, of course, science can also help with the "why." Separating science and religion is an attempt at creating a safe haven for belief and a bastion for the church, where they can still exist as science continues to erode their authority.

It is not surprising that, given the Church's steadfast approach to things like heliocentrism and the age of the Earth, people increasingly distrust religious organizations. People are smart, they will believe what is clear to them and what provides them with benefits. Science is relatively clear on things like the age of the Earth, its location in the Universe, and human evolution. We all benefit from this knowledge. When religious organizations fight against knowledge, they are fighting an uphill battle that they will lose.

Erosion of the Revealed Texts

The text of the Bible has been changed frequently throughout history. Each change, whether addition or subtraction, erodes the validity of the book as the infallible written word of God. If the Bible is perfect, then no change can be made to improve it. Every change degrades its reliability as truth about our Universe. The Bible is replete with evidence of changes and additions. It almost seems structured to highlight the various versions of history that existed in early Christianity. It is also clearly transcribed from an oral history tradition, or multiple traditions - the same stories of Jesus are often recorded from multiple people's perspective and the stories frequently differ in the telling. Sometimes they differ greatly, and sometimes the changes are more subtle.

For example, the scholar Bart Ehrman wrote about changes in the canon of the Bible. He examined a passage found in Luke 23:34 where Jesus says, "Father, forgive them for they know not what they do." Ehrman points out this verse is found uniquely in Luke 23:34 and not in any of the gospels that are describing the exact same events. The verse's uniqueness led Erhman to assume that either the passage existed in other books of the Bible and was intentionally removed or it was intentionally added to Luke in order to make a point.

The passage "Father, forgive them for they know not what they do," is sometimes interpreted as Jesus speaking to the Romans about the punishment they delivered to Jesus on the cross. Another common interpretation is Jesus was speaking to the Jews and begging his father, God, for forgiveness for the Jews for having led him to his crucifixion. The latter interpretation is in keeping with the Christian spirit of forgiveness, but downplays the idea that the Jews were at fault for killing Jesus, or in some interpretations for killing God since Jesus was God (an always-confusing lack of distinction.)

Jesus ultimately was a Jew who followed Jewish traditions. In an ironic twist, Jesus's followers became extremely anti-Jewish. They believed it was pure hardheadedness, ignorance, or even sinfulness that prevented Jews from accepting Jesus as their Messiah. Many early Christians believed other Jews were at fault for Christ's crucifixion and eventual death because the Jews had forsaken the true Messiah, Jesus, that had come as prophesied in the Old Testament. They were unlikely to want a passage in the Bible that let Jews off the hook for their actions. Early Christians may have intervened by removing the "Father forgive them" passage anywhere it appeared in the Bible in order to make the Jews more obviously at fault. They may have altered the Bible to fit their own narrative.

There are many passages in the New Testament where Jews are outright denounced and defamed. One passage, which was kept in the Bible, in John, says that Jews are actually the children of the Devil not the children of God. The idea of forgiving the Jews for killing God seems out of line with the rhetoric of the time. Their anti-Semitism ultimately culminated in pogroms bent on the extermination of the Jews (Ehrman, B. 2009.) Either way, the Bible was changed, likely, Erhman concludes, in response to an anti-Semitic movement within the Christian church (Fry, 2017).

To me, as an atheist, the interference in the biblical canon by bigots is clear evidence of fiddling with the intended message of the Bible. The changes went far beyond a simple misinterpretation of a word. The values of the New Testament were altered by the removal of the passage in Luke 23:34. What sells the point of forgiveness better than forgiving those who are killing you? There are many, many more examples of alterations of the text of the Bible. So many that it becomes difficult to understand how a literal interpretation of the Bible could be possible. It isn't clear what literal would mean considering the complex game of grapevine/telephone that was played down the millennia. Today's versions of the Bible are very different from the original text and the problems don't stop there. The books of the Bible are questionable in their authorship. Set aside the idea of it being changed and you still can't reliably expect the Bible to be written by those to whom it is attributed.

Who wrote the Bible matters tremendously. If you believe the Bible, or any "revealed text," is the revealed truth of God's wisdom for humanity, then it would help to understand those who participated in its creation. If the Bible wasn't written by the authors named in the book, maybe it can't be trusted. These days, when someone writes content like that found in the Bible we usually think of the writing as the rantings of a madman. If it was written by Joe, the schlub from down the street, the neighborhood drunk, the content would seem much less reliable.

There is a glut of evidence of the Bible's fluid authorship such as contradictions and clear errors. There are also various areas where the content and language don't line up. Within a given book of the Bible, one might find different "voices" and phrasings that were out of alignment with the language and the available knowledge of the time. Think about how odd it would be to read a story about Michael Jordan's exceptional basketball career written in Elizabethan English in the 1700s. It wouldn't make sense! These types of conflicts are found throughout the Bible, calling into question not only its authorship but even the age in which parts were written (Ehrman, 2010).

One classic example of this confusion about the Bible's authorship comes from the first five books of the Old Testament, known as the Pentateuch. Moses was originally assumed to have been the author of the Pentateuch, but over the years that view changed dramatically. As early as the 11th-century, scholars were noting contradictions in Genesis, though the scholars were mostly laughed off. The contradictions were downplayed for centuries.

In the 14th and 15th centuries, the works of "Moses" credited Moses with direct authorship, not God. In the 16th century, those studying the Bible began to float the idea that editors of the Bible had inserted information over the years. Eventually, in the 18th century, Thomas Hobbes concluded the Pentateuch was not written by Moses. His work was continued by Isaac de la Peyrere who was eventually thrown in prison until he converted to Catholicism and renounced his ideas in order to be released. Spinoza, at around the same time, was excommunicated from Judaism for espousing the idea that Moses didn't write the Pentateuch at all.

Scholarship continued and evidence mounted that the Pentateuch was authored by more than one person, over many years, and through more than one source document. In 1943, Pope Pius XII began to encourage scholars to learn more about the authors of the Bible, seeing the writers as the vehicle of God's will (PIUS XII, 1943). Today religious scholars, who are often part of the church, accept as a precept, for the most part, that the Pentateuch was written by various authors in various documents over many years. Definitely not written exclusively or in part by Moses himself.

So, how can the Bible be trusted as a source as we degrade its authorship into a hodgepodge of works? How can it be considered to be a reliable and accurate account of the events it describes? It can't. It is amazing to find a book that has persisted for so many years in popular culture, especially when it seems to have been added to and amended over the years. It is a living document, changing and being adjusted frequently to meet the needs of the times. It's evolution at its best, memetic evolution.

The Council of Nicea was a major turning point in the determination of what content ended up in and out of the Bible. The council decided on Canon during their meetings and excluded many of what are now known as the Gnostic Gospels, such as the Gospel of Judas and The Gospel According to Mary. There were many other exclusions such as the acts of Paul, and the Epistle of Barnabas. The reasons for the exclusions, while not always clear, seem to center around the acceptance of the text by contemporary Christians. The more people who accepted the text, the more likely it was to be added to the final version of the Bible. It was canonization by popular opinion.

If the Bible was compiled like that today, it would likely be up to Oprah as to what was included or excluded. Anything that Oprah didn't deem Bible worthy would then become heretical and ignored throughout history. To think the infallible word of God could be so whimsically discarded is concerning to say the least, and is another reason why it's relatively clear the Bible itself is exceedingly fallible.

Allegorically or metaphorically, many of the books of the Bible may be very interesting and worthy of a good read (maybe not the begats). It has some interesting parables that have persisted through the years, and there is a good reason these parables have existed as long as they have - the stories are moving, relatable and convey a lesson, much like the show *Friends*. That doesn't mean that we should start to worship *Friends*, though some do. Rather, we should enjoy it for what value it brings to humanity. To carry the analogy a little further, the books that didn't make it to canonization in the Bible can be seen as the "lost episodes" and should be read in a spirit of nostalgia.

All of the erosions mentioned above make it very difficult to see religion as anything other than a morphing social construct that has continued to erode and change as society has changed. The historical value of the Bible, or religion, has not eroded just because its societal value has been eroded. We can respect religious history and pay homage to our forebears, but still accept the fact that it shouldn't be the guiding principles of the world we live in today. The Bible isn't proof that God exists.

If God is immovable and eternal, then his word should be equally eternal and unchanging. It is clearly not. If God has a preferred church, the church should be the same and consistent, but it is clearly not. If priests and other religious leaders are the infallible extension of an all-knowing all-powerful God, they should remain consistent in both their teachings and their authority within Society, but they are not.

As an atheist, the erosions described in this chapter act as a very clear confirmation of what I already believe: The Church is fallible, religion is fallible, and its role in society is fallible. I am arguing that relying on such fallible books only holds us back. Humanity continues to change, and hopefully improve, as our societies mature. Meanwhile, religion seems to serve as a challenge to that maturation, slowing down the pace of change and preventing needed societal improvements. Our society, as it stands, isn't able to grow as quickly as it needs to in order to prevent its inevitable demise from things like what was described in Revelations. We need to find our way to an improved world for the sake of our children. That means discarding the yoke of religion.

What's the Point?

So here we come to an ending.

The difference between *an* ending and *the* end can be huge. I have worked on this book over the course of ten years. It was a personal exploration and proof that I can complete a large project. The end assumes the work is done. It's not. An ending is just a path to a beginning. This book was an ending and this chapter is the first step to a new beginning.

I mentioned in the introduction that I had spent time feeling militant about my atheism and that my emotions have tendered over time. I have reason to have hope now. The world, or at least America, seems to be turning a secular corner. My concern is for my children and my children's children. For their sake, I hope we can discard religion as an impediment to progress. Books like this, hopefully, keep the momentum going.

I don't know the fate of this work and ultimately I am comfortable with it not reaching the hands of masses of people, but I do hope that, if you have read this far, you have felt something, challenged your ideas, and found a home in your heart for the idea of atheism or, at least, for atheists. Most of us are very good people. We want to serve humanity and help people in need, though we suck at organizing. We want to be understood and respected for the value we want to bring to society. We are not "Godless Commies" - We are your friends and neighbors. We are millions strong, and yet often afraid of how people perceive us. All the reasons there are to be atheist, good or bad, present in this book or not, are important, but no more so than anyone else's reasons for what they believe.

We shouldn't throw the baby out with the bathwater. I am not trying to equivocate, rather I'm trying to say atheist ideas should be at the table when decisions are made just as theistic ideas should be. Books and stories allow us to think critically about the problems we face and they help us learn from the success and folly of others. Humans are storytellers and we are good at abstracting concepts and using them to make better decisions. The Bible and other holy texts have lessons to teach, it doesn't make them connected to an actual God, but it does make them useful. For example, Proverbs holds some wisdom that is apropos for this book

> "The fear of the Lord is the beginning of knowledge,
>
> but fools despise wisdom and instruction."
>
> Proverbs 1:7

> "Whoever loves discipline loves knowledge,
>
> but whoever hates correction is stupid."
>
> Proverbs 12:1

Throwing away inputs because they don't jibe with our worldview is stupid, whether religious or atheist. My hope, instead, is that this book has helped at least one person understand a version of atheism that is real for many people around the world. I want everyone to take the time to really understand the reason others have their beliefs. Understanding has immeasurable value.

I hope that at least one person reaches this ending and starts their own new beginning - a new beginning with renewed compassion and empathy for theists and atheists alike.

References

à Kempis, T. (1418). The imitation of christ. Tustin: Xist Publishing. Retrieved from https://ebookcentral.proquest.com/lib/[SITE_ID]/detail.action?docID=2128921

Abumrad, J., & Horne, E. (2007). Who am I? Retrieved from https://www.wnycstudios.org/podcasts/radiolab/episodes/91496-who-am-i

Adam, eve, and evolution. Retrieved from www.catholic.com/tract/adam-eve-and-evolution.

Add health. Retrieved from https://www.cpc.unc.edu/projects/addhealth

al-Bukhari, M. (2015). The hadith Amazon.com Services LLC.

Allies, T. W. (1896). The monastic life from the fathers of the desert to charlemagne. London: K. Paul, Trench, Trübner, & Co., ltd. Retrieved from https://catalog.hathitrust.org/Record/001590969

Anti-religious campaigns. (2016). Retrieved from https://www.loc.gov/exhibits/archives/anti.htm

Arc, J. o., & Trask, W. (1996). Joan of arc: In her own words. New York: Turtle Point Press. Retrieved from https://ebookcentral.proquest.com/lib/[SITE_ID]/detail.action?docID=5483794

Baines, W.The strange faith of donald trump. Retrieved from beliefnet.com/news/politics/the-strange-faith-of-donald-trump.aspx

Barajas, J. (2018). 3,800 artifacts once bought by hobby lobby were just returned to iraq. Retrieved from https://www.pbs.org/newshour/nation/3800-artifacts-once-bought-by-hobby-lobby-were-just-returned-to-iraq

Barbor, C. (2001). The science of meditation. Psychology Today, 34(3), 54.

Bardi, J. (2018). Atheists take heart (and office): New poll shows major support for nonreligious candidates. Retrieved from https://rewire.news/religion-dispatches/2018/12/11/atheists-take-heart-and-office-new-poll-shows-major-support-for-nonreligious-candidates/

Barker, A. (2015). Pharmacists refusing to fill spark national controversy. Retrieved from https://www.pharmacytimes.com/contributor/alex-barker-pharmd/2015/08/pharmacists-refusing-to-fill-spark-national-controversy

Frontline. ghosts of rwanda. Barker, G. (Director). (2004).[Video/DVD] Arlington, VA: Public Broadcasting Service (PBS). Retrieved from http://www.aspresolver.com/aspresolver.asp?MARC;3227852

Barro, R. J., & Hwang, J. (2007). Religious conversion in 40 countries. Cambridge, Mass: National Bureau of Economic Research. doi:https://doi.org/10.3386/w13689 Retrieved from http://papers.nber.org/papers/w13689.pdf

Bashir, M., Nelson, E. & Burbank, M. (2009). How scientology attracts celebrities. Retrieved from https://abcnews.go.com/Nightline/scientology/scientology-attracts-celebrities/story?id=8871475

Bernard Spilka, & Kevin L. Ladd. (2012). The psychology of prayer: A scientific approach. New York: Guilford Publications Inc. M.U.A. Retrieved from https://ebookcentral.proquest.com/lib/[SITE_ID]/detail.action?docID=1010621

Biberaj, E., & Prifti, P. R. (2019). Albania. Retrieved from https://www.britannica.com/place/Albania

Blanco-Elorrieta, E., Emmorey, K., & Pylkkänen, L. (2018). Language switching decomposed through MEG and evidence from bimodal bilinguals. Proceedings of the National Academy of Sciences of the United States of America, 115(39), 9708-9713. doi:10.1073/pnas.1809779115

Bordens, K. S., & Horowitz, I. A. (2002). Social psychology. Mahwah, N.J.: Lawrence Erlbaum Associates. Retrieved from http://www.loc.gov/catdir/enhancements/fy0634/2001033635-d.html

Bowker, S. A. (2000). Parents pass on religious beliefs more by word than by deed. Retrieved from https://www.purdue.edu/uns/html4ever/0003.Okagaki.beliefs.html

Brennan-Marquez, K. (2014). Is a corporation like a church? Retrieved from https://www.newyorker.com/business/currency/is-a-corporation-like-a-church

Bressan, D. (2013). October 23, 4004 B.C.: Happy birthday earth! Retrieved from https://blogs.scientificamerican.com/history-of-geology/october-23-4004-bc-happy-birthday-earth/

A brief history 1400-1994. (1996). Retrieved from http://www.cnn.com/EVENTS/1996/year.in.review/topten/hutu/history.html

Broughman, S. P., Rettig, A., & Peterson, J. (2017). Characteristics of private schools in the united states: Results from the 2015-2016 private school universe survey. National Center for Education Statistics, Retrieved from https://nces.ed.gov/pubs2017/2017073.pdf

Bryner, J. (2012). How is earth's age calculated? Retrieved from https://www.livescience.com/32321-how-is-earths-age-calculated.html

Byrd, R. C. (1988). Positive therapeutic effects of intercessory prayer in a coronary care unit population. Southern Medical Journal, 81(7), 826-829. doi:10.1097/00007611-198807000-00005

Cadge, W. (2009). Saying your prayers, constructing your religions: Medical studies of intercessory prayer. The Journal of Religion, 89(3), 299-327. doi:10.1086/597818

Campbell, B. G. (1998). Human evolution: An introduction to man's adaptations (4th ed.). New York: Hawthorne.

Carey, B. (2007, July 31,). Who's minding the mind. The New York Times, Retrieved from http://www.nytimes.com/2007/07/31/health/psychology/31subl.html?_r=1&pagewanted=2

Caroline Winter. (2012, Jul 16,). How the mormons make money. Bloomberg Businessweek, 1. Retrieved from https://search.proquest.com/docview/1040783077

Casey Chalk. (2019, Apr 1,). Judaism's nonlinear history of monotheism. New Oxford Review, 86, 28-32. Retrieved from https://search.proquest.com/docview/2214926080

Catechism of the catholic church. Retrieved from

http://www.vatican.va/archive/ENG0015/_P4G.HTM

Cohen, B. (2009). Organ failure: The arrests of rabbis who trafficked body parts uncover more complicated issues. Retrieved from https://slate.com/human-interest/2009/07/the-arrests-of-rabbis-who-trafficked-body-parts-uncover-more-complicated-issues.html

Consolata mukangango. (2016). Retrieved from https://trialinternational.org/latest-post/consolata-mukangango/

Coontz, S. (2005). Marriage, a history : From obedience to intimacy, or how love conquered marriage. United States: Retrieved from http://catalog.hathitrust.org/Record/004992938

Copnall, J. (2013, Apr 30,). Darfur conflict - sudan's bloody stalemate. Africa News Service

Cornwall, M. (1998). The determinants of religious behavior: A theoretical model and empirical test. Retrieved from https://rsc.byu.edu/es/archived/latter-day-saint-social-life-social-research-lds-church-and-its-members/11-determinants

Curtis, L. D., & Yelland, J. W. (2018). MormonLeaks: LDS church connected to at least $32B in U.S. stock market. Retrieved from https://kutv.com/news/local/mormonleaks-says-new-documents-link-lds-church-to-companies-worth-over-32-billion

Darwin, C. (1859). On the origin of species by means of natural selection (Neudr. Bruxelles 1969 ed.). London: Murray.

Darwin, C. (1871). The descent of man and selection in relation to sex. London: Murray.

Dawkins, R. (1995). River out of eden. New York, NY: BasicBooks.

Dawkins, R. (2015). Don't force your religious opinions on your children. Retrieved from https://www.richarddawkins.net/2015/02/dont-force-your-religious-opinions-on-your-children/

De Waal, Frans B. M. (2005). Our inner ape. New York: Riverhead Books.

Denning, S. (2014). Seven lessons in economic leadership from ancient egypt. Retrieved from https://www.forbes.com/sites/stevedenning/2014/08/07/seven-lessons-in-economic-leadership-from-ancient-egypt/

Dentzer, B. (2016). Religious freedom or medical neglect? idaho lawmakers take up faith-healing exemption. Retrieved from https://www.idahostatesman.com/news/politics-government/state-politics/article92784987.html

Deyo, R. A., Mirza, S. K., & Martin, B. I. (2006). Back pain prevalence and visit rates: Estimates from U.S. national surveys, 2002. Spine, 31(23), 2724-2727. doi:10.1097/01.brs.0000244618.06877.cd

d'Orsi, G., & Tinuper, P. (2016). The "voices" of joan of arc and epilepsy with auditory features. Epilepsy & Behavior: E&B, 61, 281. doi:10.1016/j.yebeh.2016.05.008

Drummond, H. (1897). The lowell lectures on the ascent of man (25. thousand ed.). London: Hodder and Stoughton.

Dye, L. (2010). Are dolphins also persons? Retrieved from https://abcnews.go.com/Technology/AmazingAnimals/dolphins-animal-closest-intelligence-humans/story?id=9921886

References

The eclectic magazine of foreign literature, science, and art. (1852). The Eclectic Magazine of Foreign Literature, Science, and Art, 25, 199-215.

Ehrman, B. (2019). Did jesus pray "Father forgive them" from the cross? Retrieved from https://ehrmanblog.org/did-jesus-pray-father-forgive-them-from-the-cross/

Ehrman, B. D. (2010). Jesus, interrupted (1. Harpercollins paperback ed. ed.). New York: HarperOne. Retrieved from http://bvbr.bib-bvb.de:8991/F?func=service&doc_library=BVB01&local_base=BVB01&doc_number=020327789&sequence=000001&line_number=0001&func_code=DB_RECORDS&service_type=MEDIA

Emily Wax. (2006, Apr 23,). 5; truths about darfur. The Washington Post Retrieved from https://search.proquest.com/docview/410093002

Ethnic cleansing in kosovo : An accounting (1999). . Washington, DC: United States. Department of State. Retrieved from http://www.aspresolver.com/aspresolver.asp?HURI;2701938

Evangelism (2009). (4th ed.) H. M. Company, Producer.

Fairbanks, A. (1906). Herodotus and the oracle at delphi. The Classical Journal, 1(2), 37-48. Retrieved from https://www.jstor.org/stable/3287085?seq=6#metadata_info_tab_contents

Feltman, R., & Kaplan, S. (2016, Jul 25,). Dear science answers your questions about evolution. Washingtonpost.Com

Fernandez, A. (2019). Tiffany haddish cries as she talks about her 'very violent' mom: I thought 'she was demonized'. Retrieved from https://people.com/movies/tiffany-haddish-cries-about-violent-mother/

Feuerbach, L., & Eliot, G. (1893). The essence of christianity (3rd ed.). London: Neeland Media LLC.

Fisher, H. (2004). Your brain in love. Time, 163(3), 80-83.

Flanagan, O. (2002). The problem of the soul. New York: Basic Books.

Franklin, C., & Layton, J. (2000). How blue tooth works. Retrieved from https://electronics.howstuffworks.com/bluetooth.htm

Fred W. Allendorf, & Jeffrey J. Hard. (2009). Human-induced evolution caused by unnatural selection through harvest of wild animals. Proceedings of the National Academy of Sciences of the United States of America, 106(Supplement 1), 9987-9994. doi:10.1073/pnas.0901069106

Frequency of prayer. Retrieved from https://www.pewforum.org/religious-landscape-study/frequency-of-prayer/

Frequently asked questions about lobotomies. (2005). Retrieved from https://www.npr.org/templates/story/story.php?storyId=5014565

Freud, S. (1927). Die zukunft einer illusion (1. - 5. Tsd. ed.). Leipzig [u.a.]: Internat. Psychoanalyt. Verl.

Friedman, R. E. (1987). Who wrote the bible? (2nd ed.). Englewood Cliffs, NJ: Prentice Hall.

Fry, R. (2017). The share of americans living without a partner has increased, especially among young adults. Retrieved from https://www.pewresearch.org/fact-tank/2017/04/06/number-of-u-s-adults-cohabiting-with-a-partner-continues-to-rise-especially-among-those-50-and-older/

Gaimani, A. (2004). The 'orphans' decree' in yemen: Two new episodes. Middle Eastern Studies, 40(4), 171-184. doi:10.1080/0026320042000240393

Ghose, T. (2013). History of marriage: 13 surprising facts. Retrieved from livescience.com website: https://www.livescience.com/37777-history-of-marriage.html

God: Biblical monotheism. Retrieved from https://rlp.hds.harvard.edu/religions/judaism/god-biblical-monotheism

Goodman, B., & Maggio, J. (Producers), & Goodman, B. and Maggio, J. (Directors). (2008). The lobotomist. [Video/DVD] Boston, MA: WGBH Educational Foundation.

Gorilla at an illinois zoo rescues a 3-year-old boy. (1996). Retrieved from https://search.proquest.com/docview/2237606833

Grim, B. J. (2017). Religion may be bigger business than we thought. here's why. Retrieved from https://www.weforum.org/agenda/2017/01/religion-bigger-business-than-we-thought/

Halbfinger, D. M. (2009). 44 charged by U.S. in new jersey corruption sweep. Retrieved from https://www.nytimes.com/2009/07/24/nyregion/24jersey.html

Harlow, J. M. (1868). Recovery from the passage of an iron bar through the head. Publications of the Massachusetts Medical Society, 2(3), 22. Retrieved from https://en.wikisource.org/wiki/Recovery_from_the_passage_of_an_ir on_bar_through_the_head

Harmon, A. (2008). Marriage. Retrieved from https://search-ebscohost-com.proxy1.ncu.edu/login.aspx?direct=true&db=ers&AN=89407079&site=eds-live

Henderson, C. W. (2008). Mindfulness meditation slows progression of HIV, study shows. AIDS Weekly, , 4. Retrieved from https://search.proquest.com/docview/2168928404

Hendrson, P. (2012). LDS church makes money by mormon donations. Retrieved from https://www.reuters.com/article/us-usa-politics-mormons/insight-mormon-church-made-wealthy-by-donations-idUSBRE87B05W20120812

Hertling, D. (2005). Management of common musculoskeletal disorders: Physical therapy principles and methods (4th ed.). United States:

History, bloody history. (1999). Retrieved from http://news.bbc.co.uk/2/hi/special_report/1998/kosovo/110492.stm

Hoover, D. R., & Margolick, J. B. (2000). Questions on the design and findings of a randomized, controlled trial of the effects of remote, intercessory prayer on outcomes in patients admitted to the coronary care unit. Archives of Internal Medicine, 160(12), 1875-1876. doi:10.1001/archinte.160.12.1875-b

Horgan, J. (2015). Can a hole in your head get you high? Retrieved from https://blogs.scientificamerican.com/cross-check/can-a-hole-in-your-head-get-you-high

Horovitz, B. (2014). Chick-fil-A wings in new direction after gay flap.

Retrieved from https://www.usatoday.com/story/money/business/2014/04/07/chick-fil-a-fast-food-dan-cathy/7250871/

Howse, C. (2008). The voices that joan of arc heard. Retrieved from https://www.telegraph.co.uk/comment/columnists/christopherhowse/3558706/The-voices-that-Joan-of-Arc-heard.html

Huberman, J. (2008). The quotable atheist: Ammunition for nonbelievers, political junkies, gadflies, and those generally hell-bound. New York: Nation Books. Retrieved from https://ebookcentral.proquest.com/lib/[SITE_ID]/detail.action?docID=845063

Hulsman. (2018). The pythia of delphi was the world's first political risk consultant! Retrieved from https://thedelphiguide.com/pythia-of-delphi-was-the-worlds-first-political-risk-consultant/

Husseini, I. (1956, October). Islam past and present. The Atlantic, Retrieved from https://www.theatlantic.com/magazine/archive/1956/10/islam-past-and-present/376245/

Jaynes, J. (1976). The origin of consciousness in the breakdown of the bicameral mind. Boston: Houghton Mifflin.

Jefferson, T. (1788). Notes on the state of virginia. Philadelphia:

Jeffrey M Jones. (2007). Some americans reluctant to vote for mormon, 72-year-old presidential candidates. The Gallup Poll Briefing, , 74. Retrieved from https://search.proquest.com/docview/200064873

Jeffrey M Jones. (2008). Americans have net-positive view of U.S.

catholics. The Gallup Poll Briefing, , 64. Retrieved from https://search.proquest.com/docview/200054353

Jeffries, M. P. (2017). The remarkable rise of tiffany haddish. Retrieved from https://www.theatlantic.com/entertainment/archive/2017/09/the-remarkable-rise-of-tiffany-haddish/538872/

Jensen, U. (2016). Economy and occupational composition. Retrieved from https://jewish-history-online.net/topic/economy-and-occupational-composition

JESSE McKINLEY and KIRK JOHNSON. (2008, Nov 15,). Mormons tipped scale in ban on gay marriage. New York Times Retrieved from https://search.proquest.com/docview/433970858

Johnson, D. D. P. (2016). God is watching you. New York, NY: Oxford Univ. Press. Retrieved from http://bvbr.bib-bvb.de:8991/F?func=service&doc_library=BVB01&local_base=BVB01&doc_number=028370384&sequence=000001&line_number=0001&func_code=DB_RECORDS&service_type=MEDIA

Jones, J. M. (2019). U.S. church membership down sharply in past two decades. Retrieved from https://news.gallup.com/poll/248837/church-membership-down-sharply-past-two-decades.aspx

Jones, J. M. (2019). U.S. church membership down sharply in past two decades. Retrieved from https://news.gallup.com/poll/248837/church-membership-down-sharply-past-two-decades.aspx

Jones, J. (2012). Martin luther, against the sale of indulgences. Retrieved from http://ramwebs.wcupa.edu/jones/his101/web/37luther.htm

Karaçuka, M. (2018). Religion and economic development in history: Institutions and the role of religious networks. Journal of Economic Issues, 52(1), 57-79. doi:10.1080/00213624.2018.1430941

Karger, F. (2017). Should the mormon church pay taxes? . Retrieved from https://www.huffpost.com/entry/should-the-mormon-church_b_13656738

Karimi, F. (2018). Here's why some businesses can deny you service - but others can't. Retrieved from https://www.cnn.com/2018/06/29/us/when-businesses-can-deny-you-service-trnd/index.html

Karkabi, B. (2008, Feb 23,). PATH OF PRAYER; looking inward; labyrinths - a centuries-old meditative device have emerged as a tool for lenten reflection. The Houston Chronicle (Houston, TX) Retrieved from https://search.proquest.com/docview/396353214

Krucoff, M. W., Crater, S. W., Green, C. L., Maas, A. C., Seskevich, J. E., Lane, J. D., . . . Koenig, H. G. (2001). Integrative noetic therapies as adjuncts to percutaneous intervention during unstable coronary syndromes: Monitoring and actualization of noetic training (MANTRA) feasibility pilot. American Heart Journal, 142(5), 760-769. doi:10.1067/mhj.2001.119138

Lambert, F. (2008). Religion in american politics. Princeton [u.a.]: Princeton Univ. Press.

Lee, M. J. (2017). God and the don. Retrieved from https://www.cnn.com/interactive/2017/politics/state/donald-trump-religion/

Lesch, A. M. (1999). Sudan, the: Contested national identities.

Bloomington: Indiana University Press. Retrieved from https://ebookcentral.proquest.com/lib/[SITE_ID]/detail.action?docID=4955925

Lipka, M. (2016). 5 facts about prayer. Retrieved from https://www.pewresearch.org/fact-tank/2016/05/04/5-facts-about-prayer/

Lipka, M. (2016). 10 facts about atheists. Retrieved from https://www.pewresearch.org/fact-tank/2016/06/01/10-facts-about-atheists/

Love. (2009). Retrieved from https://www.merriam-webster.com

Lupfer, J. (2018). Fewer couples are marrying in churches. does it matter? Retrieved from https://religionnews.com/2018/06/07/fewer-couples-are-marrying-in-churches-does-is-matter/

MacCulloch, D. (2009). Christianity . New York, New York: the Penguin Group.

Marcus, G. F. (2008). Kluge : The haphazard construction of the human mind. United States: Retrieved from http://catalog.hathitrust.org/Record/005897928

Mark, J. J. (2017). Clergy, priests & priestesses in ancient egypt. Retrieved from https://www.ancient.eu/article/1026/clergy-priests--priestesses-in-ancient-egypt/

Martinez, J., & Smith, G. A. (2016). How the faithful voted: A preliminary 2016 analysis. Retrieved from https://www.pewresearch.org/fact-tank/2016/11/09/how-the-faithful-voted-a-preliminary-2016-analysis/

Mayell, H. (2001). Evolutionary oddities: Duck sex organ, lizard tongue. Retrieved from http://news.nationalgeographic.com/news/2001/10/1023_corkscrewduck.html

McCleary, R. M. (2011a). The oxford handbook of the economics of religion. Oxford [u.a.]: Oxford Univ. Press. Retrieved from http://bvbr.bib-bvb.de:8991/F?func=service&doc_library=BVB01&local_base=BVB01&doc_number=021130082&sequence=000002&line_number=0001&func_code=DB_RECORDS&service_type=MEDIA

McCleary, R. M. (2011b). The oxford handbook of the economics of religion. Oxford [u.a.]: Oxford Univ. Press. Retrieved from http://bvbr.bib-bvb.de:8991/F?func=service&doc_library=BVB01&local_base=BVB01&doc_number=021130082&sequence=000002&line_number=0001&func_code=DB_RECORDS&service_type=MEDIA

McCracken, K. G., Wilson, R. E., McCracken, P. J., & Johnson, K. P. (2001). Sexual selection are ducks impressed by drakes' display? Nature, 413(6852), 128. doi:10.1038/35093160

Medrano, K. (2017). Hate your friend's taste in music? here's how to change it according to science. Retrieved from https://www.newsweek.com/music-brain-magnets-dopamine-stimulation-717717

Mikkelson, D. (2003). Weight of the soul. Retrieved from https://www.snopes.com/fact-check/weight-of-the-soul/

Milosevic's yugoslavia. (2014). Retrieved from https://search.proquest.com/docview/1938448400

Milton, J. (1667). Paradise lost. London:

Mooney, C. (2012). The republican brain (1. Aufl. ed.). Newark: Wiley. Retrieved from http://ebooks.ciando.com/book/index.cfm/bok_id/497868

Morgan, B., & Samso, J. (2007). Rwanda. Retrieved from https://www.pbs.org/newshour/tag/rwanda

Morris, H. M. (n.d.). The scientific case against evolution. Retrieved from https://www.icr.org/home/resources/resources_tracts_scientificcaseagainstevolution/

National Center for Education Statistics.Private elementary and secondary school enrollment and private enrollment as a percentage of total enrollment in public and private schools, by region and grade level: Selected years, fall 1995 through fall 2015. Retrieved from https://nces.ed.gov/programs/digest/d18/tables/dt18_205.10.asp

Newton-Small, J. (2016). How women secretly won the hobby lobby fight. Retrieved from https://time.com/4168895/hobby-lobby-women-congress-white-house/

Nicholi, A. M. (2002). The question of god. New York [u.a.]: Free Press. Retrieved from http://bvbr.bib-bvb.de:8991/F?func=service&doc_library=BVB01&local_base=BVB01&doc_number=009899401&sequence=000001&line_number=0001&func_code=DB_RECORDS&service_type=MEDIA

Nielsen, L. (1997). The extension, age and mass of the universe, calculated by means of atomic physical quantities and newton's gravitational 'constant'. Retrieved from http://www.rostra.dk/louis/quant_11.html

References

Nisen, M. (2016). 18 extremely religious big american companies. Retrieved from https://www.businessinsider.com/18-extremely-religious-big-american-companies-2013-6-her-companys-commitment-to-god-12

O'Connor, C. (2014). Chick-fil-A CEO cathy: Gay marriage still wrong, but I'll shut up about it and sell chicken. Retrieved from https://www.forbes.com/sites/clareoconnor/2014/03/19/chick-fil-a-ceo-cathy-gay-marriage-still-wrong-but-ill-shut-up-about-it-and-sell-chicken/#6e033ab32fcb

Okagaki, L., Hammond, K. A., & Seamon, L. (1999). Socialization of religious beliefs. Journal of Applied Developmental Psychology, 20(2), 273-294. doi:10.1016/S0193-3973(99)00017-9

O'Neil, T. (2014). Creation science: 'Old earth' vs. 'young earth'. Retrieved from www.christianpost.com/news/creation-science-old-earth-vs-young-earth.html

Pagels, E. H. (1979). The gnostic gospels. New York: Random House.

Pasley, B. N., David, S. V., Mesgarani, N., Flinker, A., Shamma, S. A., Crone, N. E., . . . Chang, E. F. (2012). Reconstructing speech from human auditory cortex. PLoS Biology, 10(1), e1001251. doi:10.1371/journal.pbio.1001251

Pastor, J., & Moen, R. A. (2004). Ecology of ice-age extinctions. Nature, 431(7009), 639-640. doi:10.1038/431639a

Paul Vitello. (2010, Mar 24,). Christian science church seeks truce with modern medicine. New York Times Retrieved from https://search.proquest.com/docview/434322695

Pew Research Center. (2014). Attendance at religious services. (). Retrieved from https://www.pewforum.org/religious-landscape-study/attendance-at-religious-services/

PIUS XII. (1943). Divino afflante spiritu. Retrieved from http://www.vatican.va/content/pius-xii/en/encyclicals/documents/hf_p-xii_enc_30091943_divino-afflante-spiritu.html

Porter, R. (2017). The greatest benefit to mankind: A medical history of humanity from antiquity to the present Fontana. Retrieved from http://www.vlebooks.com/vleweb/product/openreader?id=none&isbn=9780007385546

Prayer is 'negotiating with the lord,' says pope. (2013). Retrieved from https://www.catholicnewsagency.com/news/prayer-is-negotiating-with-the-lord-says-pope

Priestley, J. (1782). An history of the corruptions of christianity .. Birmingham: Printed by Piercy and Jones, for J. Johnston, London.

Priests in ancient egypt. Retrieved from https://www.albanyinstitute.org/ancient-egypt.html

Public's views on human evolution;2014 SRI R8584-46. (2014). (). Retrieved from https://statistical.proquest.com/statisticalinsight/result/pqpresultpage.previewtitle?docType=PQSI&titleUri=/content/2014/R8584-46.xml

Q&A: Sudan's darfur conflict. (2006, May 1,). Bbc News Retrieved from http://news.bbc.co.uk/2/hi/africa/3496731.stm

Religion and the founding of the american republic. Retrieved from https://www.loc.gov/exhibits/religion/rel02.html

Restak, R. M., 1942. (2006). The naked brain: How the emerging neurosociety is changing how we live, work, and love. United States: Retrieved from http://catalog.hathitrust.org/Record/005346772

Richard Monastersky. (1999, Mar 6,). When antlers grew too large. Science News, 155, 159. Retrieved from https://search.proquest.com/docview/197552185

Ridley, M. (1996). Evolution (2nd ed.). Cambridge, Massachusetts: Blackwell Science, Inc.

Roach, J. (2013). Swallows evolve shorter wings to avoid cars, study suggests. Retrieved from https://www.nbcnews.com/news/all/swallows-evolve-shorter-wings-avoid-cars-study-suggests-flna6C10401861

Roberts, M. B. (1986). Biology (4th ed.). Cheltenham, United Kingdom: Nelson Thornes ltd.

Rose, S., Zell, E., & Strickhouser, J. E. (2020). The effect of meditation on health: A metasynthesis of randomized controlled trials. Mindfulness, 11(2), 507-516. doi:10.1007/s12671-019-01277-6

Russell, B. (1957). Why I am not a christian. New York: Simon & Schuster, Inc.

Rwanda nuns await genocide verdict. (2001). Retrieved from http://news.bbc.co.uk/2/hi/europe/1374612.stm

S. Ratneshwar, & David Glen Mick. (2005). Inside consumption (1. publ. ed.). London: Routledge Ltd. doi:10.4324/9780203481295 Retrieved from https://www.taylorfrancis.com/books/9781134293759

Saad, L. (2018). Military, small business, police still stir most confidence. Retrieved from https://news.gallup.com/poll/236243/military-small-business-police-stir-confidence.aspx

Salat: Daily prayers. (2009). Retrieved from http://www.bbc.co.uk/religion/religions/islam/practices/salat.shtml

Sample, I. (2013). 'Determination' can be induced by electrical brain stimulation. Retrieved from http://www.theguardian.com/science/2013/dec/05/determination-electrical-brain-stimulation

Shadabi, L. (2013). The impact of religion on corruption. The Journal of Business Inquiry, 12, 102-117.

Sherwood, H. (2018). 'Christianity as default is gone': The rise of a non-christian europe . Retrieved from https://www.theguardian.com/world/2018/mar/21/christianity-non-christian-europe-young-people-survey-religion

Shinall, J., Myrick C. (2009). The separation of church and medicine. The Virtual Mentor: American Medical Association Journal of Ethics, 11(10), 747-749. doi:10.1001/virtualmentor.2009.11.10.fred1-0910

Singal, J. (2012). Why do people believe in scientology and other fringe religions? Retrieved from https://www.thedailybeast.com/why-do-people-believe-in-scientology-and-other-fringe-religions

Slackman, M. (2007). The (not so) eagerly modern saudi. Retrieved from https://www.nytimes.com/2007/05/06/weekinreview/06slack.html

Smietana, B. (2017). LifeWay research: Americans are fond of the bible, don't actually read it. Retrieved from https://lifewayresearch.com/2017/04/25/lifeway-research-americans-are-fond-of-the-bible-dont-actually-read-it/

Smilde, D. (2005). A qualitative comparative analysis of conversion to venezuelan evangelicalism: How networks matter. American Journal of Sociology, 111(3), 757-796. doi:10.1086/497306

Smith, M.Conflict myths: Bishop ussher and the date of creation. Retrieved from https://www.bethinking.org/is-there-a-creator/conflict-myths-bishop-ussher-and-the-date-of-creation

Snook, D. W., Kleinmann, S. M., White, G., & Horgan, J. G. (2019). Conversion motifs among muslim converts in the united states. Psychology of Religion and Spirituality, doi:https://doi.org/10.1037/rel0000276

Snook, D., Williams, M., & Horgan, J. (2019). Issues in the sociology and psychology of religious conversion. Pastoral Psychology, 68(2), 223-240. doi:10.1007/s11089-018-0841-1

Status of global christianity, 2019, in the context of 1900–2050. (2019). Retrieved from https://gordonconwell.edu/wp-content/uploads/sites/13/2019/04/StatusofGlobalChristianity20191.pdf

Stepler, R. (2017). Number of U.S. adults cohabiting with a partner continues to rise, especially among those 50 and older. Retrieved from https://www.pewresearch.org/fact-tank/2017/04/06/number-of-u-s-adults-cohabiting-with-a-partner-continues-to-rise-especially-among-those-50-and-older/

Stokel-Walker, C. (2017). Future - how smartphones and social media are changing christianity. Retrieved from http://www.bbc.com/future/story/20170222-how-smartphones-and-social-media-are-changing-religion

Stroope, S. (2011). Education and religion: Individual, congregational, and cross-level interaction effects on biblical literalism. Social Science Research, 40(6), 1478-1493. doi:10.1016/j.ssresearch.2011.05.001

Stroope, S. (2016). Social networks and religion: The role of congregational social embeddedness in religious belief and practice SocArXiv. doi:10.17605/OSF.IO/74PMJ

SUSAN MONTOYA BRYAN. (2019, Jun 21,). APNewsBreak: 395 claims filed in church bankruptcy case. AP English Language News (Includes AP 50 State Report) Retrieved from https://apnews.com/35d658bb86294e7ebdb20a384583cb90

Tanner, M. (2018). Religion remains powerful in balkans, survey shows.

Twomey, S. (2010). Phineas gage: Neuroscience's most famous patient. Retrieved from https://www.smithsonianmag.com/history/phineas-gage-neurosciences-most-famous-patient-11390067/

U.S. Attorney's Office. (2012). Brooklyn rabbi pleads guilty to money laundering conspiracy. Retrieved from https://archives.fbi.gov/archives/newark/press-releases/2012/brooklyn-rabbi-pleads-guilty-to-money-laundering-conspiracy

U.S. public becoming less religious. (2015). Retrieved from https://search.proquest.com/docview/2257508310

References

U.S. religious knowledge survey. (2010). Retrieved from https://www.pewforum.org/2010/09/28/u-s-religious-knowledge-survey/

Veilleux, A. (1980). Pachomian kiononia: The life of saint pachomius and his disciplines. Cistercian Studies Series, 1(45)

Vitello, P. (2009). Indulgences return, and heaven moves a step closer for catholics. Retrieved from https://www.nytimes.com/2009/02/10/nyregion/10indulgence.html

Vitz, P. C. (2013). Faith of the fatherless (2. ed. ed.). San Francisco, Calif: Ignatius Press.

Who am I? (2007). Retrieved from https://www.wnycstudios.org/podcasts/radiolab/episodes/91496-who-am-i

Williams, W. H., Chitsabesan, P., Fazel, S., McMillan, T., Hughes, N., Parsonage, M., & Tonks, J. (2018). Traumatic brain injury: A potential cause of violent crime? The Lancet Psychiatry, 5(10), 836-844. doi:10.1016/S2215-0366(18)30062-2

Winter, C. (2012). How the mormons make money :How the mormon church makes its billions. Retrieved from https://www.bloomberg.com/news/articles/2012-07-18/how-the-mormons-make-money

Winter, C., Burton, K., Tamasi, N. & Kumar, A. (2012). The money behind the mormon message. Retrieved from https://archive.sltrib.com/article.php?id=54478720&itype=CMSID

Withnall, A. (2014). Hobby lobby: Who is david green? 9 facts telling you everything you need to know about the evangelical entrepreneur. Retrieved from https://www.independent.co.uk/news/world/americas/hobby-lobby-who-is-david-green-9-facts-telling-you-everything-you-need-to-know-about-the-evangelical-9576189.html

Workman, L., & Reader, W. (2004). Evolutionary psychology (1. publ. ed.). Cambridge [u.a.]: Cambridge Univ. Press. Retrieved from http://www.loc.gov/catdir/description/cam041/2003065447.html

World: A history of tension: Serbia-kosovo relations explained. (2019, May 30,). Asia News Monitor Retrieved from https://search.proquest.com/docview/2231462072

Zimmer, S. M. (2017). Freemasonry. Retrieved from https://search-ebscohost-com.proxy1.ncu.edu/login.aspx?direct=true&db=ers&AN=87322219&site=eds-live

Made in the USA
Columbia, SC
02 December 2023

fe3e783e-beff-4da7-a946-983b708d0650R02